The Complete Book of SNOWBOARDING

K. C. Althen

CHARLES E. TUTTLE COMPANY

Rutland, Vermont & Tokyo, Japan

Published by the Charles E. Tuttle Company, Inc.
of Rutland, Vermont & Tokyo, Japan

Library of Congress Catalog Card No. 90-70431
International Standard Book No. 0-8048-7035-7

First Printing, May 1990

Cover photograph by Gwyn Howat
Designed and produced by Robinson Book Associates
Typeset by Kriff Creative Services
Printed in the United States by Thomson-Shore, Inc.

Foreword

The phenomenal growth of snowboarding is just beginning. What was once just a sport for a few pioneers has become an addictive lifestyle for thousands. All it takes is one ride through a virgin field of powder and you'll be hooked on the greatest adrenaline rush on earth. Snowboarding represents an ultimate expression of freedom and power.

Snowboarding is drawing skateboarders, skiers, sailboarders, and surfers to the hills to carve on winter's endless snow-covered waves and is proving itself to be a safe, easy-to-learn sport. In just a few short days you'll be able to master the basics of the sport and hit the slopes with confidence.

The Complete Book of Snowboarding takes you to the mountains and prepares you like a pro. Whether exploring the hills of your local resort or riding a helicopter to the top of an untamed peak, the adventure of snowboarding makes life more rewarding.

Fran Richards
TransWorld SNOWboarding

Acknowledgments

This book has been a group effort from all sectors of the snowboarding community. In the earliest stages, Georgia Lomax and John McGinnis showed the need and the possibilities for writing a book such as this.

A large questionnaire survey provided information on experiences common to snowboarders everywhere. I received information from beginners through national champions. This information included tips on equipment, learning to snowboard, and how to do tricks. A separate survey from snowboard manufacturers produced a similar abundance of information.

Many people helped by reviewing various sections of the book. Special thanks must be given to Fran Richards (*TransWorld Snowboarding* magazine) and Dean Jones III (Midwestern Snowboard Association) for reviewing the section on learning how to snowboard. Scott Downey (Sims Team) helped sort out much of the original material in the freestyle section. Jeff Van Kleeck (Mount Baker Hardcore), David DeMaio (United States Amateur Snowboard Association), and Dave Redman (Team Extreme) also helped review later versions of the advanced and freestyle sections. The equipment sections were meticulously reviewed by Mike Olson (President, Gnu Snowboards), Peter Saari (Product Development, Gnu Snowboards), Dennis Jensen (Production Manager, Mistral Snowboards), and Chris Sanders (President, Avalanche Snowboards). In addition, Dr. Jasper Shealy (Rochester Institute of Technology) and Dr. Edward Pino (Oregon Health Sciences University) reviewed the safety section.

In spite of the efforts of these experts to keep me on the straight and narrow, any mistakes are my responsibility.

Those involved in evaluating the complete draft include Kevin Kinnear (Editorial Director, *TransWorld SNOWboarding* magazine), Fran Richards (Marketing Manager, *TransWorld SNOWboarding* magazine), Frank Penzes (Editor, *Snowboarders Edge* magazine), Kevin Duncan (President, North American Snowboard Association), Chuck Allen (President, United States Amateur Snowboard Association), and John McGinnis (Burton Team).

Other people and organizations that deserve special note include: Paul Alden (Burton Snowboards), Zeno Beattie (NASTAR), Chris Copley (Burton Snowboards), Neil Daffern (Storm Snowboards), Gil de la Roza (formerly with *International Snowboard* magazine), Kevin Delaney (Sims Team), Debbie Hendrickson (formerly with Sims Snowboards), Ellen Holmes (Burton Snowboards), Eileen Hughes (Fanatic Snowboards), Miki Keller (Sims Snowboards), Dave Kemper (Kemper Snowboards), Laura Knapp (Look Snowboards), Philippe LeMay (SLM Canada, Inc.), Steve Link (Summit Snowboards), Karen Mott (Kemper Snowboards), Colin Sander (Storm Snowboards), Salina Sialega (*TransWorld SNOWboarding* magazine), Chris Stoddard (United Ski Industries Association), and Brent Turner (K2 Snowboards).

Finally, I'm sure you'll agree with me that the photographers deserve a round of applause: Glenn Daugherty, Joe Dockery, Andy Geiger, Trevor Graves, Gregg Ledge, Mike Hatchett, Gwyn Howat, Andrea Mellman, Hubert Schriebl, Greg Sheahan, Trent Roden, Brad Steward, Jim Ullrich, Jeff Van Kleeck, and Rod Walker.

K. C. Althen

Contents

Introduction

This book has something for anyone who wants to play in the snow. Which of the categories below matches your attitude about snowboarding?

Semi-Interested. If you are just curious about snowboarding, not really sure you want to try it, and think the investment of time and effort might not be worthwhile, the following few pages will give you a balanced overview of the sport.

Warning: Contents are contagious

Eager to Try It. The first chapter, "Getting Started," gives you all the information you need about equipment, with special emphasis on selecting a rental snowboard. If you have never visited a ski resort or taken lessons before, you will also find some important information on these topics. After that, the chapter, "First Runs," gives you step-by-step instructions that will teach you how to become a full-fledged snowboarder. Self-taught snowboarders usually have a very difficult time. But if you take it step by step, as outlined in the text, you will find that learning to snowboard can be surprisingly simple.

Dedicated Snowboarder. Experienced snowboarders will find three particularly helpful chapters in this book. "Getting Hot" outlines advanced techniques for different kinds of terrain. This section gives you specific points on which to focus regardless of slope conditions. It will stimulate you to develop your own theories and techniques—a life-long challenge.

"Freestyle" is filled with detailed instructions about more tricks than most nonprofessionals will ever care to master. But now you can at least find out about how to do it all.

Finally the "Equipment" chapter is filled with design, construction, selection, and maintenance information. You could eventually pick up about half of this material from your friends and the magazines over a few years—maybe. The other half you might never learn without reading this book.

Two Perspectives

Historically, skis were conceived and designed as tools for "walking" on flat snow. They do this job very well. But using two separate boards for sliding down a slope pulled by gravity is not a perfect design concept. Would you want to surf using two boards? One strong, unified board is the easiest approach. The single surface simplifies everything. This is one reason why snowboarding is so much fun.

Learning to ride a snowboard is like learning to ride a bicycle. To someone who doesn't know how, it looks nearly impossible. In the beginning, it is! But the balance and control needed to ride a bicycle or to ride a snowboard soon become second nature. Eventually it seems that it was always easy.

CHAPTER 1

Getting Started

Why Snowboard?

Snowboarding is the fastest-growing winter sport in the world. Its popularity has been increasing by 80 to 100 percent every year, and this phenomenal growth rate is certain to continue. Estimates of the numbers of snowboarders run in the hundreds of thousands for North America. No survey can keep pace.

So far, snowboarders represent less than 1 percent of the skiing population, but this is changing fast. Snowboarders come from the ranks of many types of outdoor recreationalists. And many skateboarders, surfboarders, and sailboarders are discovering this new way to enjoy winter. Snowboarding is comparable in many ways to the other boarding activities, and it is easier than skiing once you get the knack. And there's another advantage: snowboarding is a "go" almost every winter day, not just when conditions permit.

If you are a life-long skier who has become a little jaded and complacent—even bored—about skiing, that is about to change. Be prepared for a fresh and rejuvenating experience. Your appreciation of snow is about to be renewed. Your attitude and love of skiing is about to be reborn.

Can I Do It?

If you have been interested (courageous) enough to read this far, you have an excellent chance. Age is no barrier to snowboarding, though snowboarding does require some high energy at times. NASTAR (National Standard Races) conducts snowboarding races for age groups ranging from the kindergarten set to those 60 and over. Like many modern sports, the percentage of women participants is growing each year.

Young adults and children may not worry about safety statistics, but adults invariably ask "Just how dangerous is this sport?" The injury rate is comparable to that for alpine skiing. Snowboarders may have slightly more injuries, but their injuries tend to be less severe. The serious and long-lasting types of knee injuries are relatively rarer among snowboarders. The injury rate for both skiers and snowboarders decreases with experience, but the injury drop-off rate seems faster for snowboarders. The sport is still too young for comprehensive or exact numbers, but because of its apparent safety, most ski areas have opened their slopes to snowboarders. This would not have

Photo: Mistral Snowboards

Ready to go for it

happened if its safety had not been proven to ski area insurers. In just five years, the number of resorts welcoming snowboarders leaped from 7 percent to more than 90 percent. For more complete details of safety statistics, see pages 141–50.

What Do I Need to Get Started?

Equipment Preliminaries

The first thing you need is a board and instructions on how to use it. Borrowing a board from a friend is a possibility, but the size is apt to be wrong, and the bindings may need to be altered. You will also have to worry about beating up a friend's equipment (though good boards are nearly indestructible).

A better bet is a rental or demo board, which can be matched exactly to your size and weight requirements by professionals. Visit several shops if possible and talk with the staff. Pick a time when they are not too busy. In many places, avoid Friday and Saturday evenings when everyone is picking up or returning rental equipment.

A good shop, with patient personnel, will give you a "ground school" and "how-to" lecture if you are renting their equipment. Many shops have videos you can watch. But do not listen to anything anyone says about snowboarding unless he or she is a snowboarder. Smile and nod, but only listen closely to people who know—other riders.

Rental shops may also give lessons, but compare their prices with those offered at the ski areas. Lessons from your destination resort may be cheaper. Renting the board from the destination resort, however, is likely to be more expensive.

Snowboards are not cheap, so know what you want before you buy. Try at least a few different brands and models before selecting your personal board.

Selecting a Rental Board

At first, you can forego the subtleties of making a perfect match between board and rider. Your size and the board's size are the primary considerations at this time. Many other considerations are discussed in the section on boards (see pages 101–10). For now, if your weight is under 100 pounds, a 130–150 cm board is appropriate; if you are in the 100 to 150 pound range, try a 140–160 cm board; and for those over 150 pounds, a 150–170 cm board. Seventy-five percent of the models made fall into the 145–165 cm range. For starters, select one with softer flex (not too stiff) for easy turning.

Besides helping you select an appropriate board, a good rental shop will adjust the bindings for you and will make sure the board's base is prepared and waxed. When adjusting the bindings, their first question will likely be, "which foot do you put forward?" If you've skateboarded or surfed, you know. If you haven't, think about which foot you would put forward to slide across a frozen puddle. Seventy percent of riders put their left foot forward; the other 30 percent put their right foot forward. (The latter take pride in being called "goofy-footed," courtesy of the surfers.) You will probably want your front foot angled forward 35 to 45 degrees and the back one turned forward about 20 to 25 degrees from straight across the board. Pick the intermediate positions on the bindings you are using initially. Either or both foot positions can be adjusted and refined later on to fit your style of riding. See the section on bindings (pages 123–29).

The shop will also need to know your boot size. Renting special snowboarding boots is the best way to go. If the shop does not rent boots, and yours are not suitable, you may have a problem. In years past, any old boot worked, but it is now apparent that ankle injuries are the most common non-impact injury. A soft boot, for which the majority of rental bindings are designed, can be an ankle killer. Some bindings have shin straps. These can help, but even with these (or because of them) some sort of stiffening reinforcement and padding in the boot is required. To increase your comfort and safety, solve this problem before spending too much time on the slopes. See the section on boots (pages 119–23).

There is no need to worry about poles and other paraphernalia. Snowboarders don't use them. Back in the privacy of your home, dig out your wool socks and put your boots and board on just as though you were ready to take off down the hill. Protect the floor and the board with newspapers if necessary. Now is the time to readjust bindings that are too loose, straps that are too tight, safety straps with squirrelly mechanisms, and so forth. Some bindings have more adjustments than you can easily check out in the shop, and having to fiddle with them on the slope will make for a hot temper and cold fingers. It's far better to figure out the bindings on this dry run before they frustrate you or cause an injury.

Now is also the time to wiggle, lean, twist, rock and roll, and generally get the feel of being strapped onto a board. Practice some deep knee bends. Try jumping. Get used to the board's weight. Gain authority over the board. Be prepared to grin until your cheeks cramp.

Other Preparations

For Experienced Skiers. You probably have all of the accessories you need and are ready to go. A few items need to be double-checked before using them for snowboarding. Foremost, be aware that some ski goggles do not provide enough peripheral vision for snowboarding. Standing sideways requires some getting used to visually. If you are traversing a slope with your toes facing uphill and your back downhill, you have to crane your neck to see where you are going. You have to twist your head even more when you first want to turn back the other way. Goggles that block the view out of the corners of your eyes will make this more difficult. It is much easier to use wide-angle frames or sport shields.

As an experienced skier, you may be used to falling down only occasionally. That is about to end for a while. Your stocking cap, which always stayed in place before, won't last three minutes. Gloves and down parkas, which previously stayed dry all day, will be soaked. Plan ahead for such changes.

Experienced skiers naturally do not like the idea of going back to the bunny slope. But bypassing the bunny slope is the main reason that snowboarding has earned its "slam-dunk" image in certain quarters. If you head for the top of the mountain without preparation, you'll just make face prints all the way down. Be smart. No one is going to recognize you down at the bunny slope anyway. You can wear a balaclava or a face mask to hide your identity if you want. You can also secretively go at night at some resorts. Admit you are a newcomer for a little while. You will soon be improving at a hundred miles an hour, and being hungry for some "vertical," you will not have to endure the bunny slope for long.

If at all possible, do not go out your first time in icy, hard-packed conditions. If you have no choice, expect to have less fun and more bruises. Also your rate of learning will be diminished—perhaps so much that you will give up without knowing what you are missing.

For Non-skiers. Dress for winter; pile on the padding. No matter how "hot" you may be as an "otherboarder," you are about to get snow up, down, and all around. Remember how much fun it was to make angels in the snow when you were little? You will make a few more before you become proficient at snowboarding.

Use the established layered clothing method: polypropylene or other "wicking" synthetic next to the skin, wool or bulky synthetic intermediate, and an outer layer for snow and wind proofing. No cotton anywhere. Use the heaviest winter hat you own. It will double as a helmet. Heavy mittens, knee pads, and a butt pad are helpful.

Eye protection is very important. Modern sport shields (frameless goggles) give excellent ultraviolet (UV) light protection. They also will crossover for use in other outdoor sports. The same goes for good-quality sport sunglasses with retainers—but be sure they will not cut you when (not if) you fall on your face. Wide-view ski goggles are also excellent. Full ski goggles are not necessary until you reach the stage of cruising very fast or unless it is snowing heavily. However, avoid goggles that block your peripheral vision. For more details, see the section on accessories, page 129.

Lessons

It's well worth your time and money to take lessons from a professional snowboard instructor. There is little doubt that you will learn easier and faster. Just a few hours of instruction will put you well on your way to a safe and enjoyable experience.

If you do not have the money, and if you have been skateboarding, skiing, or surfing for a long time, you can combine your experience with what can be learned from this *Complete Book of Snowboarding*. Those related activities involve many skills that will transfer and be extremely helpful. This is not to say that snowboarding is the same as these activities. Snowboarding is unique—deceptively so. Still, balance is balance. And banking is banking. Videos can also help provide some instruction. For those who have skied, being able to recognize bad snow conditions at a distance and knowing your way around ski areas are huge advantages.

If you do not have a good background in skateboarding, surfing, or skiing, save up some more allowance or go back to work or go into debt, but take lessons. This is the consensus of snowboarders everywhere. (Many competent snowboarders enjoy teaching their friends.)

CHAPTER 2

First Runs

Setting Up

Finally the moment of truth has arrived. You can sense that you are about to embark on a challenging adventure. Who knows what exhilaration and thrills await you?

Make your way to the bottom of a small slope. The bunny slope at a ski resort is better than a snowy golf course or local sledding hill. Although local hills will work, there is sometimes a reduced fee for the use of bunny slope lifts compared to regular lifts. You will get your "snow legs" quickly, and you can log a lot more mileage with a simple lift. In fact, you can learn about the feel of the board and how it handles going both down the hill and up the hill on a surface lift. But don't worry about lifts quite yet. Stay on the flats.

Find a flat area and strap in the front foot only. Sitting or standing while fixing the bindings is a matter of personal preference, but sitting or kneeling will probably work best initially. Attach the safety strap first and always brush away any loose snow from inside the binding. With high-back-style bindings, do the ankle strap first, then the toe, and then the shin strap (if there is one). See the section on bindings, page 123. There is no reason to tighten the toe strap down very hard. It just holds the boot in position between the stiff sides of the binding. Similarly, do not overly tighten shin straps. Some instructors recommend that you not use shin straps, especially the one on your rear foot, when you first start. Remember the safety strap is required at all ski areas.

Before clamping in your rear foot, pretend you are on a skateboard and "skate" around on the flats. Place the rear foot between the bindings and glide for a few feet. After skating around until you feel comfortable with the new sensations, you have several options.

Option 1. Walk up a little slope. This can be done for a short way with the board still on your front foot. Simply place the board perpendicular to the fall line. The fall line is the path a rolling ball would naturally follow down the hill—the steepest course. Now side-step up the hill. The easiest way is to move your free foot up first, then bring the board up (limp up

Skating　　　　　　　**Side-stepping**

sideways). This will give you a feel for digging in the toe edge, which is an important skill to develop.

Option 2. If you don't want to side-step, you can take the board off and hike up the hill.

Option 3. After practicing a bit, you can go to the top of a bunny slope using a poma lift or rope tow, if you are familiar with them. Ride these lifts with your rear foot between the bindings, as when you were skating. (Read the section on lifts, page 28.) If you half-heartedly let the toes of your free foot hang out, or if you put your foot out reflexively to catch your balance, your foot will instantly grab and you will spin out. This mistake is a major cause of falls. *Rule: Keep both feet on the board while moving.* Do not take a chair lift at this stage.

Skate to a flat spot next to a sloping area. The trick is to find a place where you will not slide while fastening your rear binding but where you can start sliding easily by swiveling your hips or jumping once you are fastened in. The slope should be only a few feet away at the most. One way to have an ideal setup is to dig or stomp a flat area with the board right on the slope. With practice, this takes only a few moments. Once you have discovered or built this platform, fasten your rear binding. If you attach the rear binding while sitting down you do not necessarily have to have a flat spot, but then you must be prepared to go as soon as you stand up.

If you are not set up near a slope, you will have to hop, roll, or be towed to a point where gravity can take over. You can also sometimes move short distances by bending over and pushing or pulling with your hands. All of these methods are useful at times, even a lot of fun, but planning ahead is best. Now—stretch, take a deep breath, and get psyched. Big smile. You're ready to launch.

Launching

If you are positioned near where the slope breaks, or if you have dug a little platform on the slope, all you have to do is center your weight, bend your knees, hold your arms out, and throw your weight forward. Use your hips—not your back! This motion will break the board free from the level snow on which you were standing and will put your weight over your front foot. Keep 70 to 85 percent of your weight on that front foot and simply try to go straight. If your board is sideways to the hill, keeping your weight forward will pull it into a straight course down the hill. You may prefer to launch with a little jump that

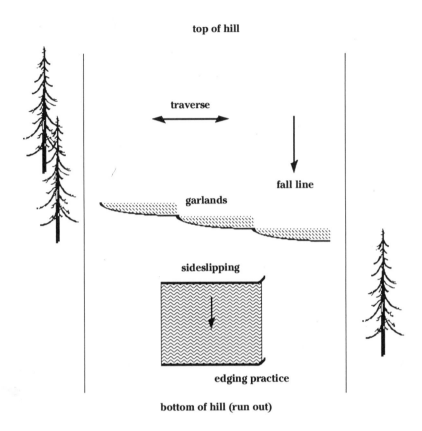

top of hill

traverse

fall line

garlands

sideslipping

edging practice

bottom of hill (run out)

Figure 1. Slope terminology

points you in the right direction immediately. Unless it is extremely gentle, this run should only be a few dozen yards before it levels off. Repeat this procedure. But at this point do not work your way up the hill so far that you will have to edge or turn to control speed.

After a few small straight runs, again practice swiveling the board while standing on the flats. This will give you a preview of the feelings involved in turning. You can then try a slightly longer run where you do some swivels on the way down. The slope should be so gentle that the swivels don't involve any conscious edging and falling down isn't a problem. If you are spending all your time getting up from falls, you are probably on a slope that is too steep or you are not keeping your weight forward—or both. These problems go together. You will learn faster on an easier slope.

Instructors vary in the amount of time spent on this stage. Some private instructors will simply gradually increase all of the variables so that the students are concentrating on turning immediately. Other instructors believe in teaching rudimentary skills so that the students know all of the basics. Edging and traversing are two of these basic skills. They have to be learned—either sooner or later.

Edging (Sideslipping)

The single most important thing to master in snowboarding is edge control. By controlling your edges, you control your speed and your direction. This is what snowboarding is all about. Fortunately, learning this control is straightforward, which is one reason why snowboarding is so much fun.

You have already started to learn the correct posture and to get a feel for balancing on a moving board. Now you must move higher up the slope, or to a steeper section of the hill, to learn edge control.

Not all edges are created equal. The preferred edge for your initial experiments is the toe edge. This is because balancing on the balls of your feet is naturally easier than balancing on your heels. The toes have far greater sensitivity than the heels. While the range of motion for both edges is equal, the calf muscles used for the toe-side edge are easier to control and stabilize than are the shin muscles, which are used for the heel-side edge. The toe side is also a little less tiring. Another consideration is that if you should overbalance into the hill, it is easier to get up and regain your balance from your hands and knees (a toe-side fall) than it is from a sitting position (a heel-side fall), especially on a shallow slope.

Forcing the toes down digs the edge into the snow and slows movement. Begin by standing with the toe edge set (dug in) and

Sideslipping on the toe edge   **Side-slipping on the heel edge**

with the board across the fall line. Keeping low with your knees bent, release the edge to start sliding. After gaining some speed, gradually reset the edge. An abrupt edge set will throw you off balance. You want to continue facing straight uphill with the board remaining perpendicular to the fall line. Slide straight down the hill on your toe edge by keeping even pressure on both legs. Try to continue this pattern of setting and releasing the edge while sliding straight down the slope. If the board doesn't stay perpendicular to the fall line, it will shoot off on a traverse (sideways). You must prevent this by shifting more weight to the side that is lagging uphill. Although this skill practice may not look so great, be patient. This same sideslipping and edging technique can take you down steep, advanced slopes if you find yourself in the wrong place.

For your next descent, switch to the heel edge. It is important to learn both ways and not to get into the habit of favoring one edge over the other. The principles are identical. The most conspicuous difference—besides being able to see where you are going more easily—is that you can use your thigh muscles to sink the heel edge in with a vengeance. Resist doing this or edging and stopping so suddenly that your weight pitches forward. If you do, you may be forced to put your toe edge down. And if you do that, you will discover the Golden Rule of Snowboarding.

Also avoid the temptation to go stiff-legged on the heel-side edge. Always keep your knees bent. "Keep low" is one of the very best pieces of advice for snowboarders.

Continue alternating edges until you have a good feel for both.

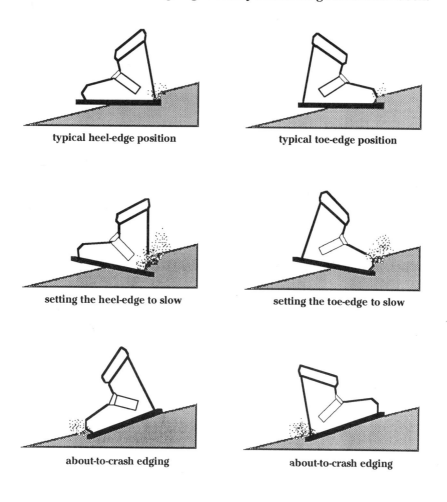

typical heel-edge position   typical toe-edge position

setting the heel-edge to slow   setting the toe-edge to slow

about-to-crash edging   about-to-crash edging

Figure 2. Edging (sideslipping)

Golden Rule of Snowboarding

Golden Rule: *Always control a snowboard with the uphill edge.* Never let the downhill (forward) edge take any weight or dig into the snow. Catching this edge will instantly catapult you onto your face or onto the back of your head. Everyone learns this rule the hard way. But if you understand the principle behind this rule, you will instantly recognize when you've neglected it, and you can keep from doing it again. Falls from letting the leading edge dig in and catch are abrupt and violent.

Very little muscular effort is required to ride a snowboard flat (not on an edge), especially straight-legged. Also a snowboard goes the fastest when it is ridden flat, but avoid the urge to do this when you are feeling lazy or tired. You have no way of controlling a flat board, and if a rut knocks you one way and the board the other way, you crash.

Golden Rule (short form): *Think edges!*

This edging action is the same as that required for stopping, so you must master this technique before attacking steeper slopes.

Falling

In falling, remember two things:

1. *Ride low.* Being low will reduce impact distance and reduce the risk to your knees by keeping them bent.

2. *Fall sideways—the direction your toes and heels point.* This protects your ankles, especially the front one.

Falls to the knees and hands, or to the rump and hands, can

be done all day long in soft snow with little consequence. If at all possible, do not go out your first time in icy, hard-packed conditions. If you have no choice, expect to have less fun and more bruises. Wear wrist guards in addition to protective padding. This is important.

Falls directly forward over the tip of the board are not too common (except from jumping), but they must be avoided. If you are losing control, getting low may allow you to recover. Also, getting forward will usually improve your chances of a recovery. Together, these two actions will at least make the fall over the side edges rather than over the tip or back of the board.

Be wary of finger and wrist injuries. You may want to protect your thumbs by putting them inside your gloves or mittens. Let your arms or trunk take the brunt of any impact. A more detailed discussion of falling is included in the section on safety (see page 146).

Traversing

Traversing means crossing the hill from side to side. A series of starts and stops in one direction creates a garland pattern. The purpose of practicing traversing is to reinforce your edging skills, to gain more speed in a controlled manner, and to improve your stopping ability.

Unlike the preliminary edging practice, you are now snowboarding. So focus on good posture: knees strongly bent, torso slightly twisted forward and shifted well over the front leg, both arms towards the front, and elbows bent. Launch as always, then ride the uphill edge across the slope until you feel like stopping or slowing. To stop or slow yourself, push or put weight on the back leg to bring the tail of the board down more perpendicular to the fall line or crosswise to your direction of travel. Do this gradually and try to maintain constant control. If you overdo it, the tail will point diagonally down the slope, and away you go again—backwards!

Heel-side traverse

Practice traversing in both directions. Go across one way on your heel edge, and return using your toe edge. When you come to the edge of the slope, you must *either* stop and maneuver the board into the opposite direction and start up again, *or* you must turn. After a few garland runs, you will be ready and able to learn how to turn.

Turning

There are three basic types of snowboarding turns: skidding turns (pivoting turns directed by the rear foot), carving turns (smooth arcs dependent upon weight shift and board shape), and jump turns (forced rotations while essentially airborne). Master skidded turns first. You will progress to the others naturally with practice and time.

For starters, return to a very shallow slope! Establish good posture, flash a big grin, and launch. With both arms out and somewhat forward, turn your head and point your lead

1. Holding toe-edge traverse
2. Weight on front foot pushes nose downhill
3. Head and shoulders rotate in desired direction. With weight on front foot, hips and back foot forcefully push rear of board around during transition to new edge
4. Control stabilized on new edge
5. Holding heel-edge traverse
6. Weight on front foot pushes nose downhill

7. Head and shoulders rotate in desired direction. With weight on front foot, hips and back foot forcefully push rear of board around during transition to new edge
8. Control stabilized on new edge
9. Holding toe-edge traverse

Diagram: SLM Canada, Inc.

Figure 3. Turning sequence

shoulder in the direction you want to turn. Look where you want to go. This motion will throw a small amount of weight onto the edge that will become active (the soon-to-be uphill one). Your weight should be mostly on the front foot already.

Exaggerate it a bit now. Steer with your back foot. That is, simultaneously push with your partially unweighted back foot in the direction opposite to that of your shoulder shift. Wow!

Although a small paragraph is all that is required to outline turning technique, this is the crucial stumbling block to overcome, both literally and figuratively. This is the key to everything. It is not nearly as easy to do as it sounds. Regardless of your background, the movements will be foreign to you initially. Learning to turn always takes considerable time and perseverance. It also takes some courage.

When you coordinate all of these actions, your turns will be fluid. In the beginning, concentrate on just where you want to make the next turn, and go for it with commitment. Although toe-side and heel-side turns may seem quite different, try to feel their similarities in terms of weight shifting and edging. The driving force always works through your hips. Keeping your weight forward will pull the board back into the fall line for the next turn. If you start to favor one direction, force yourself to work the opposite turn repeatedly until it becomes the easier and the more fun.

If you are keeping low and forward like you should, your front leg will be burning quite a bit in the early stages. Training and more advanced skills will eventually cure this problem. Don't worry; just bear it for now.

One major reason that snowboarders "lose it" during skidded turns is that they put too much weight on their back legs. They then over-rotate and spin out. This error can come from inattention, from not knowing better, from front leg fatigue, or from a fear-based tendency to lean back. Recognize any cycle of "fear of falling" and "falling from fear" and break it early. You can break the cycle by not trying to progress so rapidly. Go back to traverses or to a shallower slope. Keep comfortable to keep progressing.

After the first day or two, depending upon local conditions, you will have a feel for turning and linking your turns together. This early learning needs to be reinforced. You can continue to improve when you are not on the slopes by using visualization techniques. Close your eyes, and with intense concentration play back the necessary moves in detail. Rehearse. Use mental imagery. Also watch snowboarding videos and let your mind and muscles get involved. Think about snowboarding during all of your spare time.

Stopping

The way to stop is by holding an abrupt turn. The idea is to get the board on edge perfectly perpendicular to the fall line (like sideslipping). Snowboards have an incredible ability to

Rider: Chris Karol   Photo: Gwyn Howat

Applying the brakes

keep moving and drifting if they are kept flat. They also have an amazing ability to keep moving even on an edge if the board is pointed downhill. Since you do not have any poles, or any anchors to toss overboard, you'll need considerable finesse and skill to make the board "stick" in a particular place at the bottom of the hill.

To change an abrupt turn into a stop, apply weight to both legs, as needed, to maintain board position. Remember the lessons you learned in the earlier edging practice. Do not keep all your weight over your front foot. Experiment with different amounts of pressure when engaging and releasing the edges. As before, practice using each edge to stop.

Once you can turn in both directions and stop at will, victory is yours. You are a snowboarder.

Now start linking turns together. Make them short, make them long, make them rhythmical. Synchronize them to a musical beat. Turn, turn, turn. Try getting even lower. Don't try to add style by arching your back or experimenting with strange accents and arm movements until after you have mastered the basics.

Get these basics down solid and log as many hours as you can. The next chapter gives you the necessary information for understanding, getting around, and making the most of ski areas.

CHAPTER 3

About Ski Areas

Choosing where to go usually means going to the most convenient area, but be sure they permit snowboard skiing. (Snowboard skiing is the term preferred by the National Ski Areas Association, a member of the United Ski Industries Association—USIA.) Ninety percent of all ski areas accept snowboard skiers. If your options are open, use the considerations listed below to help you choose your location. Look for these features if you want to minimize your time waiting in lift lines and maximize your time on the slopes. It is always educational—and great fun—to check out new ski areas.

Select a ski area that:

+ is not near a town built solely as a resort
+ is not near a big city
+ is not famous (for anything)
+ has no interstate highway nearby
+ has no railroads or sizeable airports nearby
+ has other big resorts nearby
+ has recently increased its lift capacity

The more you know about a ski area, the greater your enjoyment. The following information quoted from the *USIA Skier Education Action Kit* will help you better understand what to expect and how to behave on the slopes.

The four symbols illustrated here (see p. 24) comprise the standard international trail marking system. It is extremely im-

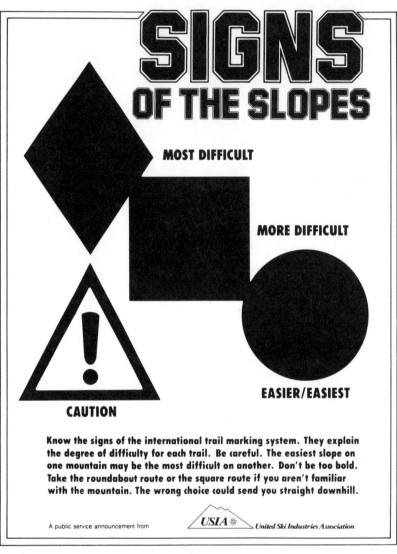

Figure 4. Trail marking symbols

portant to keep in mind that these symbols describe the relative degree of challenge of that slope or trail compared with all other trails at that particular ski area. Therefore, it is always a good idea to start off on the "Easiest" trail when you visit a new ski area, then progress to the "More Difficult" as you get a feel for the area's general degree of difficulty. Never head straight for the trails marked "Most Difficult."

The ability to do one black diamond trail does not guarantee that you can do all black diamond trails.

Know Your Mountain

When going to a ski area for the first time, get a trail map and keep it in your pocket for quick reference. A trail map will show you where the various runs and lifts are located and will give you an indication of the degree of challenge on each slope or trail. The map and international trail marking symbols will help you make responsible choices of which portions of the mountain are right for your ability. Keep in mind the day's weather and snow conditions when selecting your runs, as these can have an impact on how much you enjoy a particular run on a given day. Match your desire for challenge with the prevailing conditions.

Skier's Responsibility Code

If you see a snowboarder (or anyone else) flagrantly ignoring this code, common sense, or any other rules of etiquette, tactfully stop them or report them before it is too late.

Read and figure out the reasons for each of the rules listed in the code.

The Snow Factor

Snowmaking and snowgrooming are essential for providing snow surface dependability, a longer ski season for you to enjoy, and generally improving the quality of the snowboarding. You may find yourself scraping off icy glasses or goggles or with a spectacular frosted beard if you go under a snow gun. Therefore, extra caution and control are especially important around snowmaking equipment. Remain as far away from equipment as possible; or otherwise move through the wet spray area with extreme caution. Avoid, for example, snowguns, hoses, hydrants, pipes and valving stations. Visibility may be impaired when snow is being made. Slow down considerably. The machine-made snow surface can vary greatly. Sometimes the snow is wet, sometimes dry.

Also, be on the alert for snow vehicles used for slope maintenance. They may approach from any direction. When you see one coming, stop, wait for it to pass, and only then continue down the trail.

Snowmaking and snowgrooming do not make snowboarding safer. They simply make the snow last longer and provide a more dependable surface.

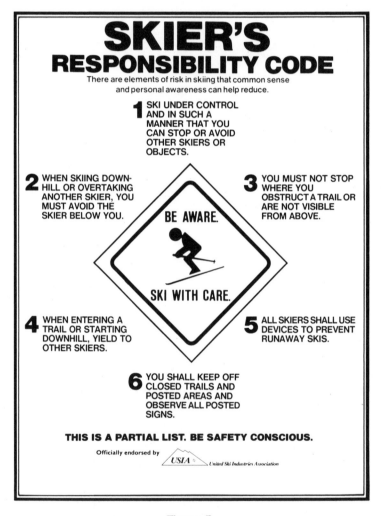

Figure 5

Snowboarding at Ski Areas

Points to Remember

+ You will get off to a better start if you do some stretching and take a few warm-up runs on easier terrain first.
+ Avoid crowded packs of skiers. This is especially important when negotiating tracks or cat-walks, and doubly so if they are icy. No matter how expert you become, you will not have poles. A board will tend to keep going on a nightmare-like path, or at least an embarrassing one, if you do not have room to maneuver. Furthermore, skiers are unpredictable. Always look ahead so you can avoid putting yourself in a tight situation.
+ Don't go snowboarding through a ski school or so close to beginning skiers that you scare them. That is a good way to lose your lift ticket. The same goes for official race courses unless you are a participant.
+ If your actions cause snowboarding to be banned at a ski resort, you may lose more than your privileges when other snowboarders find out who was responsible.

Some Final Safety Items

Trying to stop a runaway ski or board is dangerous. Shout a warning to those below.

If you should come upon, or be involved in, an accident on the slopes, you should do several things. First, alert other skiers by sticking crossed skis or the board uphill above the site. Next, note the exact location and the color of the parka the victim is wearing. Send another person or a passerby with this information to the nearest lift operator so the ski patrol can be notified.

Finally, do not move a seriously injured victim. Simply try to keep him or her warm.

Ski Lifts and Snowboards

All lifts, except enclosed ones like gondolas or trams, require that you have the board strapped to your front foot and have your rear foot free for pushing around. You must be able to move while loading and unloading from lifts. Some areas and lift operators will let you take the time to clip your rear foot in before taking a surface drag tow, particularly T-bars.

It is important to realize that having one leg free leaves the leg still attached to the board in extreme peril. When you are moving slowly, as in a lift line, there is no danger. When you are moving rapidly, as when riding a T-Bar or a platter (poma/pony) lift or sliding down the off-loading ramp of a chair lift, you must be extra careful. You must keep your free leg firmly on the board just in front of the rear binding. Having a non-skid pad between the bindings is best. *Never take your foot off the board while riding, especially in an attempt to prevent a fall.* Doing so has been known to cause broken wrists, ankles, and legs. You can easily sprain your knee when your attached leg is badly wrenched.

If you start to lose your balance, turn your board as though both feet were firmly attached. If this does not work, keep holding the free foot in place and fall just as though it were attached. Never let the board pick up excessive speed with only one foot attached! You can drag your free foot to keep the board from going faster only if you are on the flats and moving one or two miles an hour. Off-loading ramps from chairs, even short ones, are often much too steep and fast for this. If the lift operators will let you take the time to also fasten your rear foot in before taking a surface tow, do it—even if you only halfway strap in.

Platter (Poma/Pony) Lifts

Platter (poma/pony) lifts are usually used by placing a disk between your legs and letting it tow you up the hill. Because you face sideways on a snowboard, riding the platter requires a different technique than the one used by skiers. As a snowboarder, you simply grab the disk (seat) with your hands. Bend your elbows fully and lean back a little so that you can absorb the shock when the cable finishes running out and starts to pull (yank) you up the hill. Using your arms actually gives you more control and shock absorption, a real advantage when beginning. If your arms get tired, try sticking the platter under your downhill armpit. Because riding a poma lift is strenuous, you will be encouraged to progress rapidly so that you can use the

Rider: Kathy Allman   Photo: Gregg Ledge

An easy way to start

other lifts (which are normally reserved for the longer, more advanced slopes).

Keep the board flat—no edges allowed—and hang on even if it starts to send you off the track. The flat board will skid sideways, and after a few seconds you will be pulled back into the track where you belong. If you fall down halfway up, quickly roll to the side out of the way of upcoming traffic. Then ride down and get a fresh start at the bottom. There the attendant can set you up with a new platter, and you will not cause a traffic jam from rear-end collisions.

When you reach the top, always release the platter gently. Quickly skate away from the unloading area, using your free foot. Avoid loose scarves, clothing, or hair that can get caught.

T-Bar Lifts

If you are not familiar with T-bar lifts, or if you are just beginning to snowboard, you should probably try this at first by hanging on with your hands, just as you would do with the platter lift. You won't be able to do this if the lines are long and you have to ride double with someone else.

T-bars can be mastered. If you have a choice, you may want to get on the side that will allow your toes to face the center so that you can easily grasp the central stem. Quickly get into position. Flex your knees slightly, and most important, *do not try to sit down or lean back.* Stay erect. Some people put the bar behind their front leg only.

As with a poma lift, keep the board off its edges and hang on even if it appears to be sending you into oblivion. If you keep your faith and hold the board flat so that it can skid sideways, after a few seconds you will be pulled back in line where you belong. When you reach the top, the second person off should gently release the T-bar. Quickly skate or ride away from the unloading area. Remember: Do not have any loose scarves, clothing, or hair.

Chair Lifts

The chair lift is the main mode of transportation you will have to master. The basic points are:

In Line:
+ Be polite in lift lines. Everyone is watching you.
+ Have your ticket or pass visible so you don't cause delays.
+ If you have never ridden a chair lift before, alert the operator. He or she will assist you. The chair can be slowed down.

Loading:
+ Move into position as quickly as possible.
+ Hold a back pack. Do *not* wear it on your back. Secure anything that could get caught.
+ Keep looking back and grasp the chair before sitting down.
+ Sit down sideways, keep the board pointing straight, and scoot back onto the seat after lift off. Keep your free leg forward so that it isn't pulled under the seat.
+ If you fall getting onto the chair (probably knocked down from not looking), immediately get as low as you can and guard your head.

On the Chair:
+ Distribute your weight evenly in the chair.
+ Do not bounce or swing the chair. This is an excellent way to have your lift ticket confiscated.
+ For chairs without a foot rest, some people like to attach a bungee cord (18" to 24" unstretched) between the instep of the binding and the back of the chair. This relieves some of the weight and twisting on the one leg holding the board. Always unhook the cord with plenty of time to spare before unloading!

Unloading:
+ When unloading, scoot to the edge and get your weight farther forward on the chair than most skiers do.

✦ Place your weight over both feet. Immediately put your trailing foot between the bindings. Having a non-skid pad is essential. Some off-loading ramps have enough room at the top to let you put your rear foot on your board before standing up; some do not. Be prepared. Do not let your rear foot accidently drag in the snow. Do not put it out reflexively to catch your balance. You might spin out and crash. However, it is better to fall than to play wishbone with your legs.

✦ Concentrate on balancing and riding to the bottom of the ramp under control. This is one of the few times when you are exceptionally vulnerable to injury.

✦ As always, move away from unloading traffic as quickly as possible.

If you have mastered all of the techniques described in the basic learning section, and if you have learned your way around ski areas, what you need to do is add depth to your abilities. As in all sports, you can always improve. Snowboarding is now in your blood, and you are going to find yourself faced with new conditions and challenges. The following chapter will explain how to face some of these challenges, how to broaden your skills, and how to continue to grow in this great sport.

CHAPTER 4

Getting Hot

Carving and High Speeds

Carving and speed go well together. To control your board at high speeds you must carve your turns, and carved turns become more natural as your speed increases. Carved turns do not use the pivoting action of skidded turns. Alpine racers always carve because they want to minimize skidding, since skidding slows them down.

Carving

To execute a carved turn, the board must be shaped into a curve. Speed creates the necessary forces to produce this shape. However, experts can execute carved turns at low speeds with soft boards. Most experienced snowboarders claim carving is the only way down the mountain. "Carve or starve" is the motto. Learning to carve turns will give you the necessary skills for handling ice, powder, and crud, as well as speed.

Before considering technique, you need to be aware of some principles of snowboard design discussed more fully in the section on equipment (pages 101–10). Briefly, both edges of a snowboard have a slight built-in curve (sidecut). If you look very closely at your board you will observe the slightly narrower width at the waist compared to the tip or tail. Also, when you stand on a snowboard on a compliant surface like snow it bows

Toe-side and heel-side carves

down slightly (reverse camber or rocker). This increases the curvature of the edges. So if you tilt up on an edge in snow an arc will result from these two features causing the nose to point in the direction you want to turn. As an exaggerated case, imagine setting the board completely on its side in snow. If you now pushed it forward, the curve of the shovel (nose) would drive the board whichever way the tip is pointing. If you can visualize this, you are ready to carve.

Speed is closely related to carving because it increases your momentum and centrifugal force during a turn. This increases your apparent weight (g-force) and so further increases the board's curvature.

You start carving a turn by edge control and weight shift only. There is no pivot point. One of the great things about carving your turns is that you no longer need to have most of your weight on the front foot, which previously acted as the pivot point. Both legs take their share and give you a natural distribution of weight and balance.

The secret to carving a board (snow, sail, skate, or surf) is the same as for flying an airplane—match the *tilt* (bank angle), the *turn radius*, and the *speed*. Carving will have you flying—figuratively and literally. Simply tilting the board while cruising will make it turn. But bank, radius, and speed are interrelated and need to be coordinated. For example, increasing your bank angle will cause a tighter turn, but this will only work if your speed is sufficient. It doesn't take long to get a feel for how much you need to bank to hold a given turn radius.

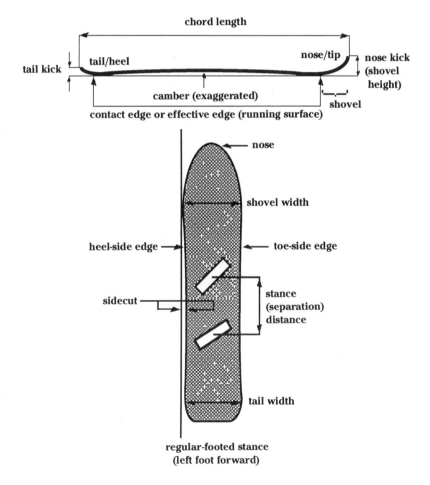

Figure 6. Snowboard terminology

It should be evident now that there are no special tricks beyond keeping your balance. Let the edges do the work. Here are some carving principles to keep in mind.

+ The sooner you switch from one edge to the other, the more secure you will be. On a flat board you go fast, but you are vulnerable to drifting, getting sidetracked by a rut, having your weight jolted off the center line, and other problems.
+ Holding your knees together can consolidate and firm up your stance. Consider a forward-tilting shim (cant plate/wedge) for the rear binding. (See the section on bindings, pages 123–29.)
+ Bending lower will permit a steeper bank for any given speed.
+ Carved turns are not as abrupt as when skidded or jumped. Speed is controlled by the amount of curvature and the length of the successive arcs as you head down the hill.
+ The more difficult snow conditions are, the more carving turns can save the day—and your neck.
+ Softer-flex boards and those with deeper sidecuts turn more sharply.

Photo: Mistral Snowboards

+ You can change from edge to edge more easily on a narrow board.
+ Asymmetrical boards are specially designed for cleaner carving.
+ The perfect carve (100 percent skidless) may be theoretically impossible, but having the sensation of a perfect carve is certainly possible.

Many more details about carving are discussed in the sections on board design (pages 101–106) and bindings (pages 123–29).

Getting Comfortable with Speed

Carving is the key to becoming comfortable with speed. Speed demands strong balance. This balance depends upon centralized weight with equal distribution on both legs, arms positioned for quick adjustments, knees well flexed, and constant edge control. This means carving turns. If you are in a competition, every little skid means lost time. For maximum speed, a long, stiff board with well-prepared edges and a base with a good wax job is needed.

Besides trying to position yourself aerodynamically (a problem on a board), hold the fall line, and look far ahead to see what is coming up. Let what is beneath you take care of itself. Anticipation is not only a key to handling the turns but also large bumps with lips. The well-established technique of pre-jumping is vital if you want to retain maximum speed over some bumps. As in skiing, or even sailboard racing, air time is lost time. If you can forcefully launch yourself in front of a knoll or bump, you

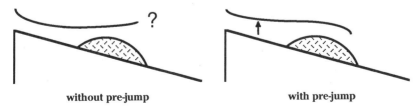

without pre-jump · · · · · · with pre-jump

Figure 7. Benefits of pre-jumping

can land just beyond the lip. This way you avoid becoming airborne indefinitely. You maximize contact time and have contact and control just where you want it the most—on the downhill, steeper, accelerating side of the bump. This is very important. For the vast majority of bumps and irregularities, however, use your legs like shock absorbers. Compress and extend as necessary to keep your center of gravity and your vision at a constant level.

Deep Powder

Going for deep powder is the ultimate for many slope connoisseurs. Powder is light, quiet, smooth, sensuous, rhythmical, and—of course—impact resistant. The down side: it is slow and requires unfamiliar technique. Although it is fun to fall into, it can be a pain getting yourself out of, cleaned off, and going again if you happen to sink into bottomless powder.

The great news is that snowboards have design features that

Rider: Chris Karol   Photo: Gwyn Howat

make them natural powder machines. The single surface eliminates the possibility of crossed or divergent tips, both of which are constant worries for skiers. The large area and easy rearward balance of a board lend themselves to natural, high-riding cruising.

The preferred boards for deep powder are those with a high shovel in front and average-to-stiff flex, like all-around boards. Such boards usually have slightly rounded, kicked tails; the upturned tail in effect reduces resistance from the rear edge, lets the tail sink, and makes edge changing a little easier.

To discover the thrills of powder for yourself, begin with shallow powder and progress gradually. Fairly steep slopes (where the snowgroomers cannot go) are fine because the plowing action of the board will slow your acceleration. To keep the nose from diving, keep your feet equally weighted, or perhaps slightly back. Keep your side-to-side balance well centered. Rhythmically tilt your body and let the board carve naturally. Knowing how to carve a snowboard will be a great asset even though the edges are inactive (in the normal sense) in bottomless powder.

Deep powder presents a situation where you not only want to think edges, you also want to feel the entire bottom surface of the board. It is possible to use pivoting turns or a combination

Caution

Speed, ice, and crud may cause a lot of bruises and sprains, but hitting a tree can be fatal. Do not enter dense or remote stands of trees alone. Stay in communication with your friend(s)—by shouting if necessary. If you are knocked unconscious, you can suffocate. If you are injured, the ski patrol may never find you.

of both pivoting and carving turns. Unweight for the turn initiation or the change of edge, hold the curve, then rebound with a measured rhythm. A rhythmical motion will increase your appreciation of the smoothness of powder.

There are a few other secrets to keep in mind. Maintain constant fall line speed and never slow enough to "sink out." Avoid flats even if they are short. Turns must be well anticipated and not hurried. It is this continuous and symmetrical linking of the turns that gives the characteristic, uniform patterns observed in powder. Minimize excessive movements such as flailing arms. Be rhythmic; do not crank and grind.

If you do acquire a taste for powder, you'll discover that you can never find enough. Go high; go north side; go lee slopes; go early after snowfalls; and go in the trees. A board is so maneuverable in powder that you will soon be finding untracked patches.

The difficulties in handling powder are elemental. It is more a case of learning not to fight the bulk, of foregoing wasted motions, of concentrating, and of working *with* the snow instead of against it. Dream of champagne powder and frozen smoke.

Moguls

Shah Jahan, the builder of the Taj Mahal, once owned a magnificent diamond that was named the Great Mogul. Over the years, dark and sinister tales have surrounded this gem, and it has now been mysteriously missing for more than 200 years. Today, if you want to discover great moguls, look for the signs showing black diamonds.

When skiers find themselves dropping down a steep slope, say 30 degrees or more, they vigorously check their speed. This action dishes out a pile of snow and deposits the snow in front. The action of successive skiers reinforces both the trough and the mound. These semipermanent obstacles slowly migrate up the hill, in theory, as the downhill sides are shaved and the resulting snow is plowed up from the troughs and onto the uphill sides.

Most riders would agree that frozen moguls are not much fun, but snowy ones permit outrageous antics. Snowboards, with their high maneuverability, really add to the enjoyment. Fundamental to mastering moguls is the ability to crank a turn in either direction at will. If you are anxious to develop your turning skills, moguls are the place for you.

Begin in shallow bumps on a shallow inclination. They go together. The classical approach is to begin sliding up the uphill side. Near the peak, the ends of the board will be partially unweighted or free from the snow. Unencumbered, you can easily pivot and then check your speed while skidding or slicing down the back side. Dead ahead will be another bump on which to repeat the performance with a new bearing.

Experts use various techniques to make this simple pattern successful. The number-one technique is strong knee flexion to absorb the high points. This compressing motion is crucial. The idea is to keep your upper body relatively quiet, especially in the vertical sense, and to have your legs act like shock absor-

Rider: Joe Sawyer   Photo: Mike Hatchett

bers—fairly extended in the troughs and compressed on the mounds. Do not bend your back. Keep your arms forward. Compressing permits you to "catch" the downhill side of the mogul as you extend your legs for speed control. It also means there is less vertical momentum to absorb because your center of gravity is already lowered and does not have as far to fall on the downhill side.

An expert uses judgment and forethought to plan his or her course through a field of moguls. In a run that is wide relative to its traffic load, the moguls will be gentler towards the edges. In a narrow run, the moguls may be uniform right to the edge of the tree stand, but often one border will have received more sun and therefore be softer, or one side may have less sun and therefore have fewer spots worn through to dirt and rocks. If you find running the edge of a run worthwhile, stay balanced but be ready for turns toward the center and away from the side, where a branch or snag may suddenly seem to jump into your path.

If conditions are too extreme, you can repeat successive turns in one general direction on a long traverse for as far as possible. This approach will improve your control and stability on any terrain. But remember: zig-zagging down the fall line while keeping the head and shoulders at a constant level shows the most style. The only way to make those apparently split-second decisions is to anticipate your course by looking two or three moguls ahead at all times. In addition, you must glimpse the overall pattern. Try to take each mogul no matter how miserable it looks. Occasionally cruising off on a traverse will give you a breather and remove you from the main traffic. Sometimes turning on every second mogul or twice on a big one will give a better cadence and rhythm to the run or to part of a run. You must adjust your technique depending on the different sizes and shapes of the bumps. For example, be wary of those with gentle uphill sides and cliffs on the downhill sides. Here the usual mistake is not to compress enough on the easy side while in front of the lip.

Most of the foregoing discussion covers average conditions. If you are one of the lucky early-comers to a mogul field after a heavy snowstorm, run the ruts. This is an adrenaline rush. Do not mess with the bumps; slalom the grooves. The board won't hang up like long skis do, but you have to do the shimmy at double time. No problem. You're getting hot!

Ice

Ice comes in many different degrees of hardness. Some so-called ice is just hardpacked snow that is so old the flakes have fused. This kind of ice does not require melting, that is above-freezing temperatures, to form. Grey ice is a term applied to even more solid stuff, and blue ice is like frozen water. Blue ice is best attacked with ice skates, so avoid it. A small patch can be carved or skidded, but it may require some fancy moves to recover control after crossing the danger zone.

Grey ice can be negotiated with practice, and all ski areas, East and West, can have greater or lesser amounts at times. You cannot totally avoid it, so, it is best to learn how to handle this unforgiving surface.

The most important requirement on ice is sharp edges. (See the "Tuning" section, page 110.) And edge control is what han-dling ice is all about. Wearing high-quality boots is also impor-tant. Hard boots with plate bindings provide the strongest edge control. But a rigid edge can cause chattering, which means that the board periodically loses its grip. Some claim that soft boots provide less-rigid edging and so discourage chattering. In-dividual technique, experience, and practice are clearly all factors.

The usable edge on a board is only about 40 percent of what skiers have to work with. This means the pressure per unit length of a snowboard is about 2½ times greater, and this extra pressure is a "good news/bad news" proposition. The good news is that regardless of how icy it is you can always dig in a little. The bad news is that if you are skidding a turn instead of carving it, for example in trying to stop quickly, a board is susceptible to chatter. This is hard on your ears and the fillings

in your teeth. In certain very cold conditions, the extra pressure can quickly chew up the P-tex base of your board.

Handling ice is not so much a question of using special techniques, but of making no mistakes. You cannot carelessly put your hand down on turns. You cannot lean too far back. You cannot relax straight-legged. You cannot lose speed control. Losing speed control is easy, even tempting, if you say to yourself, "I'll slow down when I reach . . . ." This is how and where those impact injuries occur. Wear protective gear if you are facing off against serious ice.

If you encounter frozen ruts, even on a narrow track, it is safest to cut them at an angle and on an edge—that is, to keep carving. Otherwise you will be trapped and shaken like a bowling ball in a gutter. Beware if the trail is narrow or crowded with skiers. Also, if you are traversing alternating patches of icy hard pack and softer snow, closely watch for the changing conditions. Coming from ice and hitting softer snow throws you forward. Coming from snow, the board may suddenly cut loose when you first hit ice. Experienced skiers have an advantage in being familiar with this phenomenon. If you haven't skied much, try to be extra-sensitive to this problem. Experience is the only answer.

One final consideration: when conditions are icy, you may not be able to hold as steep a slope as your skiing buddies.

Extra-Steep Slopes

Up to a point, increasing steepness does not require any special techniques. At first, carved turns give way to skidding turns as braking becomes essential. At this stage there are only two small problems. First, when on a toe edge and perpendicular to the fall line, it becomes difficult to see what is below. Second, unless the snow is deep, standing on the slope demands a more strenuous edge-set. A 45-degree slope will produce an automatic 45-degree edge-set, which would normally be radical. Because snowboards are so wide, the leverage the legs must combat is considerable.

When it gets really steep, a new technique will force itself upon you—the jump turn. This is the fun part. It entails compressing (bending the knees), unweighting (springing up), and rotating. All of this requires excellent anticipation and aggressive commitment. You are watching where you are going, or trying to, so the rotation actually begins with your shoulders, proceeds with your trunk and hips, and ends with the board. An important principle to visualize is that of moving the front of the board downhill. (Do *not* visualize swinging the tail uphill and around.) Often it also helps to focus on some small irregularity in the snow as a starting point. So focus on a specific patch, crouch as you hit the point, look where you want to land before leaping, and go for it.

You do not necessarily have to become airborne. The idea is that when braking becomes absolutely necessary, the turns, semi-carved or otherwise, must be quick, abrupt, and accurate. What a trip!

When considering an extreme or unfamiliar couloir (gully) or

cliff face, be wary. For example, if there is ice under a shallow layer of powder, you may have trouble holding an edge. Consider carefully which edge to begin on for each situation. You can maintain more control in an unstoppable slide if you are on your toe edge. You can also "read the snow" by letting someone who hasn't read this book go first.

Alpine Racing

If you are seriously interested in racing, examine all of the skiing manuals you can find on competitive racing. Skiers worked out all of the angles years ago. They invented it. Then gain experience by entering every possible contest for which you are eligible. NASTAR and other similar programs are great for training. Both the North American Snowboard Association (NASBA) and the United States Amateur Snowboard Association (USASA) sanction races.

Racing traditionally includes, in order of increasing speed: slalom, giant slalom (GS), and downhill. Slalom courses are the shortest and have the tightest turns. They require great finesse. Downhill courses are the longest and have the most widely-spaced turns and gates. They require the most courage, but not necessarily the most aggressiveness. GS and the newer "Super-G" are intermediate courses and require both guts and skill.

Slalom

For regular *slalom,* a single, flexible pole marks each turn, so bashing each pole permits the straightest line through the course. To an observer pole bashing may seem to be the racer's

Rider: Kerri Hannon   Photo: Glenn Daugherty

main preoccupation, but to the racer this is incidental. It is simply a necessity to protect the body, face, and head while focusing on the turns. The turns are everything. Each one must be perfectly anticipated and cleanly executed. Anticipation allows you to set up high above the pole, compress and shift onto the new edge set, hold the groove with minimum skidding, drive past the pole, and accelerate out of the carve in time to set up for the next gate. After anticipation, it is a battle of concentration and fluidity.

Although straight lines drawn from each pole to the next define the shortest course, this is not the fastest course. To preserve speed, the turns have to be carved curves. By shifting the center of each curve slightly uphill for each gate, the overall pattern is kept, but now you have a little more margin for error at the gate. If you lose your hold on the snow momentarily you will go wide or below the gate—not inside or over it. You are in a position to risk sweeping by much closer. This is why you need to initiate your turn above the pole. You want to straighten the curve and regain speed as soon as possible after the gate. A flat board will accelerate the fastest in a straight line before angling off on the new trajectory. As always, stay low when possible and control the arms with restrained, purposeful movements.

Giant Slalom

Giant slalom and *Super-G* are large and extra-large versions of regular slalom, as their names indicate, but they have something more—speed. The optimum course to follow is not as well defined as in slalom, so it requires more judgment and experience. Also, the gates are composed of double poles with banners, so they are less forgiving. These sturdier gates combined with the extra speed mean that the flagrant pole bashing seen in regular slalom has to be moderated. Trying to splinter unbreakable poles does not add to speed. Apply the same principles of high turns, clean carves, good posture, and strong

accelerations out of the turns. Disciplined technique developed from practice and more practice is the answer. GS is tough.

Downhill Racing

Downhill racing represents an ultimate expression. The scattered gates are almost irrelevant except for marking the route of the course. The need for equipment in perfect condition becomes obvious, although it is crucial in all competition. Helmets, lycra suits, special boards, and special waxing are all part of the scene. Good luck charms are too. The basic techniques for speed were highlighted in the earlier section on carving and speed. Top snowboard racers now run downhill courses at extreme speeds, and you cannot learn how to do that from a book. Living on the slopes is the only answer.

Getting Air

Start small. It is possible to get airborne on the flats by simply hunkering down and jumping up (*ollie*-ing). Realize that air can be addictive, and a "go-for-it" attitude, or ambitious friends, can easily lead you into jumps that you could handle better with just a few more weeks' practice. Resist going for something radical and finding yourself crumpled out with an injury. Maybe it will only be a small pull or wrist sprain, but it can still spoil your attitude for a while. Your high ambitions will backfire, and your rapid progress will come to a standstill. Start small, but do not stay small. Grow.

Launching

What are the things you want to think about? For a start, perfect control and posture. If you have grown careless about the positions of your arms, get them up. Have them forward so that they remain within your peripheral field of vision and are ready to act as stabilizers to correct your balance. Next, focus your attention on the lip of the jump and lower your stance as you approach it. Use your legs, not your back. Shift your weight back so that your rear leg has its share by the time you hit the lip.

Then jump straight up as you hit the lip. This is why you must have your weight on both legs. Spring straight up in relation to gravity—not in relation to the angle of the jump. (Of course this is impossible if the lip is extremely vertical.) Don't go off stiff—stay flexible. If the landing is nice and steep, you might need just a little forward rotation so that your axis is more perpendicular to the slope at touchdown.

If you try going off a jump that is too big for your current level of expertise, you won't be eager to jump and do it right. Fear and reluctance may cause you to hold back in an effort to minimize the consequences of your actions. This holding back results in the common error of landing heel first with your weight too far back. No control. Splat. Grunt.

While You're Airborne

During flight, make sure you keep your head up and focus on the landing area. One important thing to remember is this: keeping your head upright and on an even plane stabilizes the inner ears' balance and preserves visual orientation. Watch a cat falling (as if thrown) or a hawk putting on a fantastic aerial display. Their heads remain steady and square. Also keep your main axis upright. Keep your arms high. You need to bend your knees again slightly to anticipate the landing. You can do numerous tricks at this stage, and these are discussed at length later on in the special section on freestyle (pages 61–100). Move on to extravagant antics only after you have an intuitive understanding of the principles involved.

The next few paragraphs contain some principles of physics which are difficult to follow. If you are not interested in these, jump to the next section, "Landing."

Principle number one: Once you leave the ground, your center of gravity will be in a fixed trajectory (parabolic). No amount of

Racing his shadow to the spot

flailing will change the perfectly smooth arc of your center of gravity. This is entirely defined by your take-off speed and angle.

Principle number two: You will also have some fixed amount of rotational momentum about an axis through your center of gravity. This rotational (angular) momentum will be divided into three components corresponding to the three dimensional axes through your body. The total amount cannot be changed once you are airborne. Your rotational momentum can be transferred to some extent between axes, and it can be superficially counteracted as described below.

Rotational momentum must be distinguished from rotational *velocity*. You can vary the rate you spin through the air easily. The more you pull the mass of your body, especially your arms, inwards toward the spin axis, the faster you will rotate for a given amount of rotational momentum. The farther you extend your arms, the slower you will spin. Recall how figure skaters can control their speed in a spin with their arms and their free leg or how gymnasts can control their rate of somersaulting by controlling their tuck. It is not important to understand the physics, but it is vital that you have an intuitive feeling of what is going on. Only in this way will things work for you rather than against you.

Because of the sideways stance of boarding, it is complicated to analyze the different axes of rotation, but it is possible to counteract or to increase the rotation about each axis slightly. All you need to remember is that if your pitch axis is off (somersault axis if you were on skis), you can compensate a little by fully extending your arms and circling them in the direction of rotation you are trying to counteract. For example, if you are rotating forward and the board is turning down too much, make clockwise circles with your left arm and counter-clockwise circles with your right. If your roll axis is off (tilting sideways towards an edge on a straight jump), you can hold your arms parallel with the board and circle them for minor adjustments. In theory, you can compensate about 10 to 20

Beware

The small jumps formed by skiers at the sides of runs are sometimes "sucker jumps." This is because many of the novice skiers experimenting with these little jumps end up cratering the back side. You merrily see a nice lift-off point, take it, and discover too late that the back side is nothing but a pit. All you can do is deepen it.

degrees on each rotation of your arms. Also in theory, you can maximize the effect by having the top of each circle even with your shoulders and the bottom of the circle about 60 degrees lower (as measured from the shoulder). In other words, make big circles aimed somewhat downwards, not just straight out from your body.

All of this is fine in theory, but what this discussion should reinforce is that the moment you launch, the outcome is largely determined. You can twist, tweak, and contort into all sorts of freestyle positions and still land fine if the take-off is correct.

Landing

To stick the jumps reliably, you need to land with the board parallel to the slope and your weight distributed *just as though you were already cruising.* If the snow is soft or wet, however, the board may tend to plant itself for a split second and to throw your weight forward. Practicing under different conditions is the only way to learn how much to compensate for this variable factor. Think mainly about getting the board parallel to the slope, keeping your head and back fairly square to the slope, absorbing the impact almost entirely with your legs (not with your back), and using your arms as balancers.

Professional freestyle skiers have discovered that the optimum landing slope has an angle of about 37 to 38 degrees. This angle is much steeper than you might expect. The more elevation you achieve, the more important it is that you find a place to absorb the energy of your landing gradually. The trouble is, if the far side of the jump slants down at a good angle, you may not be able to see if the jump is clear of obstacles. Always check to make sure your jumps are clear! This is what friends are for. Likewise *never, never stand, sit, or lie around under a lip or knoll where you are invisible to uphill traffic.*

Large Tuck (ready for grabs)

Tricks

One elementary trick you can do is a *Tuck* (Gelände). This entails bringing your knees up as high as possible. You will soon discover that you can only do this by bringing your shoulders and upper body down to meet them. Your center of gravity is constant, so bringing some weight up means bringing an equivalent amount down. Action and reaction. If you are in a tuck and you put your legs down, your head will go up in a relative sense. If your jump is not true, doing a tuck might correct it. But it may also exaggerate any error or somersaulting tendency.

Another elementary "air" you can try is a *Twister*. While aloft, straighten out your whole body and twist the board to one side. You will see that the only way to achieve this action is to twist your shoulders and arms (not necessarily your head) in the opposite direction. Action and reaction. If you want to have all of your body twisting or spinning in the same direction, you have to generate the rotational momentum while you are on the ground and still have something to push against.

Spinning, where everything rotates, is quite different from doing a Twister. With spinning, realize that if you wind-up too far in advance of the lip, you will lose some of your recoil force and you will be more likely to hit the lip locked in a funny pose. Likewise, if you take off a fraction of a second too late, you will find yourself doing part Twister and part spin, and your landing will be hard to predict. (See the "Freestyle" section for 360s, Fakie 180s, and others.)

If you have become a competent snowboarder, you can best improve your advanced skills by exposing yourself to different snow conditions, slopes, and ski areas. If you find yourself repeating the same old runs in the same old conditions, your development will be stifled. Naturally, racing specialists need to repeat familiar runs in order to learn how to shave a few more seconds from their time, but if you ever feel you are bored or that your development is stymied, the following chapter has a cure to get the electricity flowing again—freestyle.

CHAPTER 5

Freestyle

It is another day on the mountain. Your body is screaming for high-energy excitement. You want to be free. You have style. You know the cure. This section will expand your awareness of the possibilities.

Keep several things in mind as you check out this catalog of tricks and maneuvers. First, no listing can be 100 percent comprehensive. Only the most important tricks are included. A small sampling of exotic tricks are briefly presented just to show the potential range for inventing tricks. But from a practical point of view, these are never seen. Some tricks, like the handplants, are very difficult to perfect. And if your area, like many others, does not have a halfpipe, you will find these basic tricks more than enough challenge. Improvise.

Second, there is no universally accepted terminology, and there are geographical variations in the names. Sometimes tricks have a popular name as well as a descriptive name. For example a BFM can be called a Fakie-Back Flip-360-Hand Plant and vice versa. Inventing your own name(s) may be half of the fun. In a sense, each time a stunt is performed it is somehow unique—just like the snowflakes that make it all possible.

Third, some of these tricks are fairly safe, some are somewhat dangerous, and some are definitely dangerous. Be smart and learn progressively. *Do not attempt a trick for which you are not yet ready.* Those included here are not arranged in order of difficulty. Professional instruction and protective gear are ap-

propriate for some of the more extravagant maneuvers, so don't put yourself out of commission even before the training clinic begins.

Finally, a simple trick done with nice height and clean style has a lot more appeal than a "double gobble-de-gook with a half-twist" that ends in a crumpled heap.

Some Definitions

Quite a few of the airs, grabs, and so forth were first established by skateboarders, and in an ongoing tradition much of the terminology derives from these "original shredders."

Note: All of these definitions are written for the regular-footed stance. If you are one of the many goofy-footed readers, simply reverse all necessary directions.

Backside turn   In a halfpipe, for regular-footed, a right or clockwise turn. A misprint? No. In this case, if your backside faces the wall while turning, it is a backside turn. It is irrelevant which edge, if any edge, is used. Note that for regular-footed, the left bank (facing downhill) would be used for any simple backside turn. For goofies everything is exactly the opposite. Just for the record, skateboarders consider the backside hand to be the front, forward, or leading hand. That is the left hand for regular stance and the right hand for goofy-footed riders. Again, this is not a misprint. This is the ready hand for grabbing the heel edge—the backside. But because all of this is confusing, I call the front hand the "front hand."

Boned	Executed with an extended or straightened leg. Try to momentarily lock the knee or, at least, make it look like it is locked.
Fakie	Riding backwards. Anything done tail first (180 degrees around).
Frontside turn	In a halfpipe, a left or counterclockwise turn done off the right wall facing downhill for regular-footed riders.
Grabs	**Crail**. Grabbing the front toe edge with the rear hand. **Method**. Grabbing the front heel edge with the front hand. **Mute**. Grabbing the front toe edge with the front hand. **Nose**. Grabbing on or near the nose. **Nuclear**. Grabbing the front heel edge with the rear hand. **Stale**. Grabbing behind your body with your rear hand to the heel edge. **Tail**. Grabbing on or near the tail.

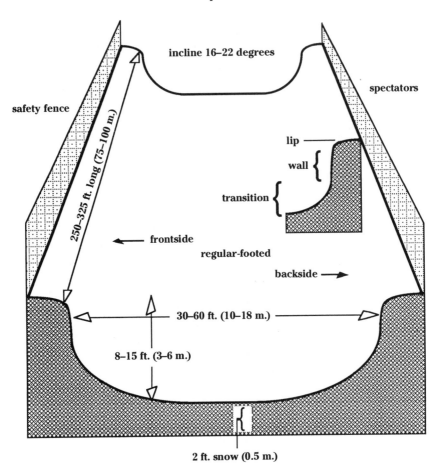

top of run

incline 16–22 degrees

spectators

safety fence

250–325 ft. long (75–100 m.)

lip

wall {

transition {

frontside

regular-footed

backside →

30–60 ft. (10–18 m.)

8–15 ft. (3–6 m.)

2 ft. snow (0.5 m.)

Other NASBA specifications:

transition	1.5 to 3 meters
inner height of wall	1.5 to 3 meters
vertical	10 to 30 cm.
platform width	1 meter minimum
flat	7 to 12 meters

Figure 8. Competition halfpipe

Ollie	Jumping the board into the air, either flat-footed or by rocking back on the tail and throwing your weight forward.
Quarterpipe	Single wall.
Rail	The side edge of a board (all kinds).
Sad	Boning the front leg.
Style	Individuality. Style includes such things as arching the back and using the free arm to extend the line of the curve.
Transition	In a halfpipe, the curving slope rising up from the flat area to the wall.
Tweak	To push to the limit. To become as distorted as possible.
Wall	The steep side of a pipe.

Note: The freestyle tricks are divided into three different areas. "On the Slopes" covers tricks that do not require getting airborne. "Off the Jumps" covers those that require some air but that can be landed in the same direction of travel. And "In the Halfpipe" covers those tricks that normally take-off and land on the same wall and transition. To be sure, you can launch straight out of a halfpipe on a kicker (a small jump) and you can do some halfpipe tricks on the slopes, in a mogul field, on a cornice, and so forth. These divisions are for convenience. Remember: The tricks within each subdivision are *not* in order of difficulty.

ON THE SLOPES

Fakie (Backwards)

This is a skill with tremendous potential and is needed for many advanced tricks. This is also a skill worth developing for its own sake. For example, use it to start off again after a miscalculated stop that leaves you facing the edge of a run. Or to back out of trouble near a lip or obstacle. Or simply for variety, and the "what the —" affect it has on some newcomers and skiers.

Once you have started to ride Fakie a little, you can immediately start to do ground 360s. Actually, doing a 360 in the snow is easier than sustained Fakie riding. Simply do a complete revolution (which may or may not include a pause while facing uphill at the 180 degree mark). Start slowly on the flats because this demands some unnatural weight shifts and edge changes when you are first learning it. A flashy and fun trick for all ages. Clockwise is probably easier, if you are regular-footed. After you finally figure it out, go for it in the opposite direction and start crashing all over again. Isn't snow great!

Rider: John McGinnis   Photo: Andy Geiger

Wheelie

Pretend you are doing a Wheelie on your bike. Romp back and try to ride the tail for as far as you can go. The boards are tough enough to take it.

Nose Wheelie
(Nose Roll/Nose Slide/Nose Ride)

Skid around 180 degrees so that the board is going tail first; then throw yourself forward over the tip of the board as though going into a hand stand. Support yourself with the stable triangle formed by your two hands and the tip of the board. Keep the tail of the board up as high as possible for effect. Although you will be going backwards, this is a relatively easy beginner's trick. You can make it a lot tougher by trying it with only one hand or with no hands, but don't expect to hold it for long.

OFF THE JUMPS

It is assumed you have already read the general section on getting air (pages 53–57). This has some important and useful information in case you skipped it.

Sidekick (Mule Kick)

This is just a little maneuver to throw in quickly on a small lift-off. Good practice.

Heel-Edge Grab

This is probably the grab you want to start with. Simply go into a tuck as described in the section on getting air. Then grab your shin the first time to get used to not having both arms free. The next time, grab your boot. After that, grab the heel edge of your board. You've got it! Some instructors prefer to teach students to first slap the bottom of the board, and then progress to a toe-edge grab from underneath. One advantage is that you can definitely clamp onto the toe edge, whereas a heel-edge grab is less secure. Another advantage is that it teaches a posture closer to that of a Method Air, which is the usual goal. At smaller areas, all of these grabs are loosely referred to as Methods. In any case, wear heavy-duty gloves or mittens. This should come much more naturally to freestyle skateboarders than to skiers.

Rider: Craig Kelly   Photo: Rod Walker

Toe-Edge Grab

This is another fundamental grab. While comparatively straightforward as shown here, this same grab reappears in halfpipe tricks. As a Backside Air, the Indy Air, it is quite a different maneuver.

Freeriding version of Method Air

Method

A Method Grab is a heel-edge grab with the front hand on the forward section of the board. If the grab is done with the *back arched* and both knees facing more or less downwards, it is known as a Method Air. When done in its classic form as a Backside Air in a halfpipe, it is important to get the board as high as possible. It is impressive when tweaked with a lot of air. For style, remember to extend the free arm.

The basic grab reappears in many tricks.

Halfpipe version of Method Air

Mute

A grab to the forward toe edge with the front hand is a Mute. The Mute grab appears in many tricks, and is often done off a backside wall when it is then called a Mute Air. Of course it can, and should, be boned.

One extreme variation is to tweak it into a Japan Air, if you have enough height and experience. In this case, the board must be extended far behind you about back- or head-height.

Crail

Use the trailing hand to grab the forward toe edge for a Crail.

Nose Grab

Grab the nose with your front hand. Since you want to keep your body axis straight, this means you have to get that tip up high. Be sure to release the nose in time to get the tip back down fully so that you land with the board approximately parallel with the slope and with your axis in balance. For style, bone your back leg. This photograph shows one with a Frontside Air in a halfpipe. Another opportunity for this grab is as a One-Handed Rocket (see page 79).

Rider: Craig Kelly   Photo: Rod Walker

Nuclear

A grab onto the forward heel edge with the rear hand is known as a Nuclear. It also appears in two-handed tricks in combination with other grabs.

Tail Grab

Grab across the back or near the tail. This picture shows a tweaked variation in a halfpipe using the heel edge. Tail Grabs to the heel edge can be further described as Stale (as here) or Nuclear depending upon whether the trailing or front hand is used. Using the front hand on the toe edge instead of the back hand makes it a Crail Tail Grab. There is also a Double-Handed Tail Grab done by bringing the tail of the board up behind your back after a straight jump and grabbing on both sides. This is one for those drop-offs where the landing zone is steep and you do not have to worry about positioning the nose before impact.

Rocket

Normally this is a two-handed grab with both hands near the shovel. If only one hand is used, it is still considered a Rocket (or Rocket Air), if the board is forward and vertical. This is a great one to do while freeriding, and it is a simple trick, at least compared to some of the following. Rockets come in other versions by changing the usual grabbing position. For example a Back-Handed Rocket is done by twisting your back towards the board and facing uphill. In this position you can put your front hand on the toe edge near the nose and, with greater difficulty, your rear hand around onto the heel side. It is also possible to do a Tail Rocket by pulling the board around into the Rocket position with the tail facing upward instead of the nose.

Cross-Rocket

Cross the trailing hand to the heel edge (Nuclear) and the leading hand to the toe edge (Mute). As with a regular Rocket, you will want plenty of elevation to have time to complete it and still get in position for a graceful touchdown.

180-to-Fakie

Launch (or ollie) and twist 180 degrees to land going backwards. This sounds simple enough, but do not try this until you have gained considerable proficiency riding backwards. You can begin to learn this and the following maneuver at very modest speeds and on easy terrain simply by jumping hard enough to get airborne.

The opposite move is a Fakie 180. Hit the jump Fakie (going tail first), and rotate 180 degrees to land conventionally. If you are regular-footed, it will probably be easier if you turn this in the clockwise direction. Some prefer to be on a slight toe edge rather than just flat for the initiation.

This trick can also be ollied on flat ground with a little muscle power. In still another version, while on a heel edge, you can lean back (downhill) to lift the nose up while swinging the nose so that the board pivots on its tail to bring you around. Normally this is done at a moderate speed, but if done a bit faster, you will be vaulted for some air.

The obvious way to do a rotational jump is to do a 360. In many ways this is more natural, and it is the same as a Helicopter in regular skiing.

Rider: Jeremy Allen   Photo: Jim Ulrich

360 Mute Air

You will need some height and holding your arms out will look wilder, but tucking them in will significantly aid in spinning. It is also vital that you keep your back as erect as possible during this maneuver. The twisting motion must be very strong and well timed. Be sure that you have read the general information under the section "Getting Air." In other words, if you want to get around in time, pull your arms in tight unless you have a lot of altitude. The secret is to be almost halfway around by the time you leave the lip. Throw your arms out on landing to check the rotation and to help catch your balance.

Any aggressive person can start this trick. Only skilled ones can finish it.

Remember that many of the tricks just described can be combined for extra flair. For example, it is possible to do a 360 Mute Air. It is also possible to do some sequentially. For example, there is a snowboarder's version of the skier's Daffy. This is a Nose Grab followed by a Tail Grab all in one air. Another combination is a Two-Handed Tail Grab-180-to-Fakie. The list is endless.

IN THE HALFPIPE

Most halfpipe tricks, both airs and handplants, can be categorized as backside or frontside maneuvers depending on which wall is used. An exception is a straight Air-to-Fakie. Shoot up either wall and launch without changing the board's direction. Unless you are already proficient at riding Fakie, this will be more difficult or at least more unnatural than a simple Frontside or Backside Air. But in any case, it provides another starting point where you can start small and work up to where it becomes impressive.

Air-to-Fakie

Rider: Jeff Fulton   Photo: Jeff Van Kleeck

Backside Air

The basic Backside Air involves hitting the left wall (right wall for goofies) and turning back onto the transition. A Backside Air often includes holding your heel edge with your front hand. Initially you may want to remain compressed. Other Backside Airs include the Method Air and the Mute Air as defined earlier. Whatever the grab, if any, you now do it with a half turn in the air so that the landing comes back down high on the transition.

Another Backside Air mentioned earlier with the trailing hand holding the toe edge between the feet is the Indy Air. With the hand grip in this position, it is difficult to straighten either leg. In principle though, it is possible to straighten the rear leg on the way up or the front one on the way down after passing through the high point. At the high point, you should be leaning forward into the pipe with the board as high as possible.

Frontside Air

The basic Frontside Air involves turning frontside (right wall for regulars, left for goofies) while possibly holding the toe edge with your trailing hand. Bone your rear leg for added style. It is also possible to bone the front leg depending on where you initially grab.

In dream country

Smoke Jumper

Rider: Tara Eberhard   Photo: Hubert Schreibl

Rider: Jason Ford   Photo: Trevor Graves

Serious carving

Rider: Amy Howat   Photo: Gwyn Howat

How smooth can you get?

One way to get a lady's attention

Spectral frontside

Demonstrating what handplants are all about

Squaw Valley Method

Lien Air

This Frontside Air variation is named after skateboarder Neil Blender (*Lien* is *Neil* spelled backwards but is sometimes seen as *Lean Air*). Hold the heel edge with your front hand in front of the front boot while turning. Bone the rear leg (soft boots) or arch your body (hard boots) for maximum effect.

Slob Air

This, with its variations, is a popular way to do Frontside Airs. In its basic form, you grab the toe side with your lead hand. Once you have that mastered, you can begin to experiment with complications. The easiest is probably the Double-Handed Slob done by grabbing with the back hand up alongside the front hand.

In all of these airs, you will want to get the board into position as fast as you can in order to get into that snapshot pose and hold it for the longest time possible without jeopardizing your landing.

Roast Beef

Doing a Frontside Air, go into the Slob Air position but grab the heel edge between your legs with your rear hand. Extend the back leg as usual. It is important to bone your back leg as much as you can. Even for someone who has never before seen such freestyle tricks, this will give a much better impression.

Stale Fish

Use your rear hand to grab the heel edge between your feet again, but instead of going through your legs, go around your back leg.

Canadian Bacon

In this variation, you need to grab forward from the Stale Fish position through your legs to the toe edge. This is not the sort of trick you can expect to see at your local hill. Here are a couple of other professional stunts just for the record. The Swiss Cheese is done by doing a Slob with the front hand and a Roast Beef-like grab with the back hand, but the back hand is shifted further forwards in front of the front heel. Another is a Spaghetti Air done by doing a Slob with the front hand and a Canadian Bacon-like grab with the back hand, but also shifted further forward near the front hand. It is a Double-Handed Slob with a knot.

Alley Oop

This is an air that is counter-rotated from the expected direction and therefore requires a full 180 degrees of swing or more. For example, for a toe-side Alley Oop you shoot up the toe-side (frontside) wall, but then with a strong push you pull a Backside Air to everyone's amazement. This is comparatively easy if done without a grab. In general, for this and most other halfpipe tricks, you will normally want to approach the walls fairly straight-on, which also means with plenty of speed to carry out your plan. Stay low, using your knees and not your back.

As you might expect the reverse of this maneuver is a heel-side Alley Oop. This is done by doing everything on the backside wall. It is also possible to do an Alley Oop-Mute, for example, by hitting the frontside wall, grabbing Mute, turning backside, landing, and riding it out.

A 360 can also be done in a halfpipe which is similar to that described in the "On the Slopes" section, but now you are returning to the transition from which you initially departed, so you have to land it Fakie. You are landing in essentially the same position from which you launched, but now will be sliding back down the hill.

The regular 360 may seem strange because you have to land it going backwards. One cure is to hit the wall going Fakie to begin with, so that by doing a 360 you land in the normal direction. This is a Fakie 360 or a Caballerial (after Steve Caballero, the professional skater). If you can keep sufficient speed, balance, and orientation, the regular 360 followed by a Fakie 360 makes a good "one-two" combination. You can mix and match and change spin directions in endless combinations. If a Caballerial is combined with a Mute Grab (lead hand on toe edge) it becomes a Gay Twist, a trick for professionals.

Another 360 Air from Fakie is the Indy Gay Twist. In this case you grab Indy (rear hand on toe edge between your feet). In theory, the Fakie 360 might be combined with a Slob or other position if the rotation were done frontside instead of on the normal backside wall, as for the previous two tricks.

Another rotational air is the 540. In this case it is landed facing in the normal direction. Something to look for at pro competitions. The first ever freestyle 540s were popularized by the ice skater Axel Paulsen who performed them in the 1880s (landed Fakie on one foot). Some pros can do 720s.

Two-Handed Invert (Handplant)

This is the basic handplant/invert to start with. Make sure your hat and sunglasses are strapped on. Hit the backside wall straight on with enough speed to carry you up and over the lip with just the right amount of momentum to stall you in a handstand. Learning this speed is purely a matter of trial and error. The idea is to sort of cartwheel so that your hands remain on the lip but your hips and legs continue on upward permitting you to extend upside down. Initially do not worry about getting fully extended until you get your general bearings and get a feel for the return twist and fall back onto the transition. Use your upper body strength to hold or even help push your torso back into its normal upright position. You have to get the board back under you and twisted so that it meets the snow again in a reasonable position, allowing you to continue. Use your arms to push your body away from the wall and to get your weight immediately over the board at touchdown. Focus on getting most of your weight on your rear leg initially for good balance, and remember that the higher you are on the wall at touchdown, the more speed you will have for the next hit. If you can stall (freeze in position) a Two-Handed Invert like a gymnast's handstand, it is equivalent to the skateboarders' Ho-Ho Plant.

One-Handed Invert

Approach the backside wall just as in the two-handed version, but immediately catch all of your weight on your rear arm so that your leading arm is free to grab the board as though it were a skateboard about to be lost. Common ways are to grab the toe-side edge between your feet or the heel-side edge in front of the front foot. You can add flare to some Handplants by straightening the rear leg (boned) or the front leg (sad).

A slight variation is an Andrecht. Do a backside invert and grab on the backside edge behind your back and between your feet. This trick is named after 1970s skateboarder Dave Andrecht. This can also be done with the front leg boned (sad). It then is called a Sad Andrecht (or Bonedrecht). An Andrecht where you grab the heel edge with your front hand between the legs is a Stelmasky (Stalemasky).

For the basic Frontside Invert, approach the frontside wall fairly straight-on while staying low and compressed. Hit the lip still compressed and push the board over your head as you roll back onto your front hand. Grab between your feet on the toe-side rail. Finally push off the wall with your arm and pull yourself in again to get the board back onto the snow. This is a very difficult trick to do well.

Layback (Lay Air)

Hit the lip turning slightly frontside or preferably straight on. Plant the rear hand and then immediately start turning a Frontside 180. The front hand can remain free or grab Mute (front hand on the front edge) or between the legs. When first learning this, do not worry about getting completely inverted. Support your upper body with your back arm until you can get your feet underneath you.

J-Tear

Hit the frontside wall fast in a fairly compressed posture. Lean back as you approach the lip. Pretend you are going to do a back flip with a strong twist. You have to rotate as the board and your legs go up and beyond the lip leaving your shoulders and head at a fairly constant height just above the level of the lip. Get both arms down and out to make the catch. Getting out of this is fairly conventional. Fold your lower body to get everything under you, and push off with your hands to get back on top and sail down the transition. This trick was invented by professional rider Mike Jacoby. This is an advanced maneuver that should only be attempted by experienced freestylers. In fact, this trick was originally in jeopardy of being outlawed because of its similarity to inverted aerials. Now by definition, if your hand touches the lip before your board goes below your head, it is not considered an inverted aerial. Inverted aerials are illegal at all U. S. ski resorts.

There are many other extravagant Handplants. In fact if the trend follows the skateboarders' lead, there are dozens of subtle variations which can come into and go out of popularity as time passes. For a hardcore freestyler though, Handplants will always provide a source of variety to a routine, interest, and of course, a challenge.

The next chapter changes gears and brings you back to earth. Knowing your equipment is as vital to snowboarding as it is to all other sports. The earlier you learn about equipment and the more you know about equipment, the better off you'll be. By now you are likely to have developed a distinctive and personal style, and you know what kind of snowboarding you like. But you cannot achieve and make the most of your snowboarding goals unless you know how to get the most out of your snowboarding equipment.

CHAPTER 6

About Equipment

Snowboard Design

Graphics

The first thing you see when you look at a snowboard is its art work. It is almost impossible not to be influenced by the graphics, but smart snowboarders know they can easily individualize and customize a sliding billboard with spray-paint, reflective tape, or stickers. Before you customize a board, clean it with paint thinner or mineral spirits to improve adhesion. Very fine sandpaper (400+) also works. So, before dismissing a well-designed board just because you think it is ugly, consider making a graphics design statement of your own.

Size

The other obvious feature is the board's size. Size is important because the board must match your size and weight. Here's an approximate guide for the weight to length relationship:

under 100 pounds	130 to 150 cm
100 to 150 pounds	140 to 160 cm
over 150 pounds	150 to 170 cm

This scale is for beginning and average riders.

As mentioned earlier, about 75 percent of the boards sold are between 145 and 165 cm in length (57 to 65 inches). With experience, aggressive riders may want longer boards, especially if they are interested in speed or competitive racing.

Manufacturers commonly measure length on the basis of the material length (as if the board were rolled flat) rather than the chord length. (See diagram on page 37.) But for comparing board lengths, the most valid measurement is the length of the contact edge.

A large shovel in front and a kicked tail reduce a board's effective running length considerably. These features are helpful for riding in soft snow, performing freestyle tricks, and increasing maneuverability. Longer edge contact provides greater stability. Actual edge contact relative to a board's total length varies from 70 to 80 percent, but it can go up to 90 percent or more on competition racing boards. It is difficult to determine what these percentages are while shopping, and manufacturers' published edge contact values do not correspond to those from independent testing laboratories. Also, when snowboards are compared by test riders, the expected relationship of stability and ease of turning compared to the length of the edge contact are sometimes overshadowed by other factors, particularly flex and shape.

Flex

Flex refers to the stiffness of the board; it is just as important as the length. Soft flex results in a more maneuverable board, which means turns are easier to initiate, quicker, and sharper. Softer boards are easier to learn on, and this is why many freestyle boards, being soft, are excellent for beginners. The trade-off is that stiffer (alpine) boards promote stability. An aggressive carver riding on hardpack needs a stiff board that can bite into the snow and hold an edge. The pattern of flex also affects a snowboard's performance. For example, a soft nose is desirable for easy turn initiation and keeping the tip up in light powder—but a soft nose can twist and turn and cause trouble in heavier snow. You may appreciate stiffness in the tail while on a Super-G course but not while riding the bumps or in a halfpipe.

Torsional rigidity is related to flex, but it specifically refers to a board's resistance to twisting along its long axis. Stiffer is often claimed to be better when it comes to torsional rigidity.

It is customary to talk about flex as if it were distinct from length and width, but from a design viewpoint they are always related. The flex of a board varies approximately with the cube of its length. Therefore a board only 26 percent longer would be twice as flexible if not built to be correspondingly stiffer. For any given board, the stiffness can be calculated as N/cm (Newtons/centimeter or force/distance). Snowboards average about 100 N/cm on this standard scale of measurement. Soft ones are generally below 85 N/cm; stiff ones are over 115 N/cm. Understandably, if you ask a salesperson for such comparison statistics, you are bound to get weird looks. Instead, hold the board upright with its tail on the floor. Hold the tip with one hand and push in the center with the other to see how much it gives. Now at least you look like you know what you are doing. This is an interesting way to compare snowboards, but it is nearly impossible to gauge a board's actual performance in this way. The salesperson should be able to tell you which models are stiffer or softer within a brand line and possibly between brands. However, the best––and ultimately the only—way to judge performance is to test the board yourself on the slopes under varied conditions.

Width and Sidecut

Increasing the overall width of a board helps create stability and reduces the likelihood of boot overhang and drag. It also increases the muscle tension you must use to keep your board on edge—most notably on long traverses. Narrower boards reduce this strain and improve your ability to move from edge to edge quickly.

Sidecut also influences a board's stability and quickness. Sidecut refers to a board's slightly narrower midsection compared to its nose or tail. The midsection may be 1.5 to 3.5 cm (0.5 to 1.5 inches) narrower. Sidecut values may refer to both sides, as here, or to one side only. For comparison purposes, however, values given as the radius of a circle with the same curvature as the arc of the sidecut are best. For example, an eight-meter-radius sidecut is designed to turn sharper than one of 11 meters, everything else being equal. Note that each side of an asymmetrical board may have slightly different radii.

High-speed boards have only a slight sidecut because they are designed for straight tracking and shallow turns. A sophisticated competitor should try to match the sidecut and natural turning radius of a particular board to each specific racecourse.

Sidecuts can be of varying shapes and they can be custom shaped by hand or determined mathematically. A *radial* sidecut is one that is equivalent to the arc of a very large circle. A *progressive radial* sidecut has a large radius circular cut followed by a slightly smaller radius cut near the center. A progressive radial sidecut is approximately the same shape as a quadratic sidecut. A *quadratic* sidecut is mathematically equivalent to a parabola and is similar to the curve formed by a suspended cable such as a telephone line. Some consider this more-refined curve superior because it more closely matches the path of a carving turn. This is because the quadratic sidecut is shallower at the ends, and this compensates for the normal flex pattern, which is comparatively stiff in the midsection and softer towards the ends. With the extra bowing at the ends, a smooth circular arc is again the final result.

Camber

If you place a snowboard on a level surface with no weight on it, the center section will bow slightly off the surface (0.2 to 1.1

cm; 1/8 to 1/2 inch). This is the camber of the snowboard. This up-bowed shape is related to a snowboard's flex. A stiff board with strong camber will be able to bite hard along its full length to the very ends of the board. A board has camber for that reason—to transmit the force of your weight to the ends of the board, improving your ability to hold with the full length of the edge. Soft flex results in more down-bowing from your weight (reverse camber or rocker). A four-foot board with two inches of reverse camber has more curvature than a four-foot board with one inch of reverse camber. Also, a two-foot board with one inch of reverse camber has more curvature than a four-foot board with one inch of reverse camber. So short, soft, deeply sidecut boards carve more sharply. Long, stiff, slightly sidecut boards track straighter and allow higher speeds. At high speed, small inputs have large effects. Centered camber is best for easy turning. Rearward camber is best for powering out of a curve at higher speeds.

Symmetry

Until recently, almost all snowboards were symmetrical. Now there are many models available with edges of different lengths (tail is cut on an angle) and with asymmetrical sidecuts for the toe- and the heel-side edges. In a symmetrical board, the side-cut is normally correctly positioned for the toe edge, but as the heels are angled farther back on the board, the weight position-ing on the heel-side edge is slightly too far back. The asymmetri-cal design shifts the entire heel edge and sidecut rearward, where it belongs. Boards may also have slightly asymmetric noses. Strangely enough, an asymmetrical design makes carv-ing on both edges the same, so the result is symmetry in performance. Some freestyle boards are becoming more similar (symmetrical) in the tip and tail to provide equal performance in both directions (riding forward and Fakie).

Shape

There is more to designing the shape of the shovel (front tip) and the tail than you might suspect. A high shovel planes up and clears obstacles more easily. A low shovel has less resistance to air and especially to snow. These effects of drag are important in competitive racing. A low shovel also has less resistance to sideways motion when slicing through snow and has less swing weight. Swing weight refers to the resistance of the board to rotating, especially in the air. The force required to do an aerial 360, or just a simple jump turn, depends not only on the weight of the board but on how much and how far that weight is distributed from your turning axis, namely at the tips. A sharply turned-up shovel, regardless of its height, permits greater contact edge length. A gradually turned-up tip, regardless of its height, provides smoother riding.

A turned-up tail reduces a board's effective tail area. A "kicked" tail normally has rounded corners. This kind of a tail improves your maneuverability in powder and the bumps, and enables you to ride Fakie and pull off various freestyle tricks. A flat tail normally has square corners and has maximal edge contact. It has a better profile for racing and recreational carving.

Taper or *taper angle* refers to the tail width relative to the nose width. High taper (that is a wide nose with a narrower tail) allows for easier turning but reduces the board's holding power.

Many of the features described above (flex pattern, sidecut, width, swing weight) can be positively or negatively influenced by the position, spacing, and angles of the boot bindings. See pages 126–28 for what to consider when mounting bindings.

Snowboard Construction

Core

If you take a flat stick and bend it in a circle, the inside surface will experience squeezing (compressional) forces, and the outside surface will experience stretching (tensional) forces. At some theoretical point between the two surfaces of the stick, it is being neither compressed nor tensioned, neither pushed nor pulled. The inside has it easy; the outside does all the work. The closer to the surface any part is, the more abuse it must endure.

Snowboards are built from the inside out. The core materials for most boards are either foam (polyurethane) or wood, and sometimes both. Polyurethane dampens vibrations better than wood and is a little easier to work with. Wood is stronger, more resilient, and more durable. Manufacturers use various kinds of hardwoods, and, occasionally, softwoods (which have a high strength-to-weight ratio). There are too many variables involved to reliably compare wood to polyurethane in terms of weight, uniformity, or expense.

A few snowboards have cores of aerospace materials (titanal or aluminum alloy) in a hollow honeycomb construction. This is combined with solid alloy sheets, hardwoods, rubber, and/or glass laminates for the final sandwiched construction.

The earliest snowboards were made entirely of wood. Horizontally laminated boards, in which a number of sheets were sandwiched together, were the norm for many years. This style of construction is like that of skateboards. Then in the mid-1980s, snowboards began to be constructed like alpine skis. Today the wood is only deep inside and it is vertically laminated in many small strips side by side. This construction makes snowboards more lively and very strong.

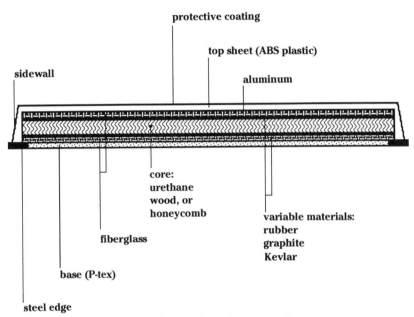

protective coating

top sheet (ABS plastic)

sidewall

aluminum

core:
urethane
wood, or
honeycomb

variable materials:
rubber
graphite
Kevlar

fiberglass

base (P-tex)

steel edge

Figure 9. Snowboard construction

Laminations

Manufacturers use all sorts of strong materials to surround the core. Fiberglass is the standard material, and it is usually applied as a woven cloth impregnated with resin. This composite can be laid up in different geometries and in different states of curing from completely wet and uncured to completely cured and stiff like a sheet of glass.

The bottom of the board, which handles the stretching mode, is often further reinforced, sometimes with carbon graphite fibers. These fibers can be woven with the fiberglass or oriented along the long axis. Kevlar is another synthetic that may be applied along the board's bottom length. Both of these materials are lighter and much stronger than fiberglass, and dampen vibrations better. Both are also harder to work with and more expensive. Kevlar is the strongest. Rubber (or its equivalent) is sometimes incorporated as the ultimate dampener. It also improves the bond between adjacent layers because it is a flexible interface.

The topside of the board requires several additional layers. Aluminum plates are common, either for binding retention or as protective pieces in the nose and tail sections. Almost all top sheets today are made of ABS plastic (acrylonitrile butadiene styrene). ABS comes in many grades, but it is chosen for its high impact strength. Above this, to protect the ABS and the graphics, manufacturers add one to five layers of lacquer for a clear finish, for greater scratch resistance, and for ultraviolet light protection. Sidewalls to protect the core are usually made of epoxy, phenolic, or ABS plastic.

Base

The base and the edges come between the board and the snow. The base is always polyethylene (P-tex), but it can come in various types. Most boards use grade 1000. This is a high density, high molecular weight formulation that can be extruded, which is a relatively inexpensive process. This grade does not absorb as much wax as the ultra-high molecular weight bases do. Ironically, boards with this type of base do not need to be waxed as often as do those with sintered bases.

The specialized bases (grades 2000 and up) have ultra-high molecular weights (UHMW) but are actually less dense in their final form. This combination makes them tougher and more resistant to rock damage. Bases having ultra-high molecular weights are "sintered" rather than extruded; this process gives them greater porosity, higher wax capacity, and lower density. Sintering involves forming the plastic into a block from a powdered state by means of high pressures and heat. During sintering, microscopic pore spaces remain. Other materials, such as graphite, can be mixed in with the batch. Graphite, in contrast to polyethylene, conducts electricity, and many believe that this results in less static charge buildup, especially in dry, cold conditions. Regardless of the reason, boards with sintered bases are the best gliding and the fastest *if* you conscientiously wax and maintain them. If you tend to neglect waxing and maintenance, a board with a plain extruded base may serve you better.

Edges

Modern snowboards have steel edges; these edges are required on all snowboards used at ski resorts. High-quality steel edges have a Rockwell hardness of 48 or more. Cracked edges may be slightly less hard. Manufacturers use cracked edges mainly for curved sections of the board. These have the advantage of isolating vibration better than continuous one-piece edges.

Tuning Your Board

To keep your snowboard the high performance tool it was designed to be, three primary areas require your attention. These are: base preparation, edge preparation, and waxing. Even a new, fresh-out-of-the-box board should be checked out in all three aspects.

Preparing the Base

Some professionals recommend removing any factory wax from a new board. It has protected the surface during shipping but may not have been applied conscientiously or be correct for your local conditions. You can remove it with commercial wax removers (xylene) or with acetone if you are concerned. There is no easy way to know if your new board needs rewaxing. Many of the better boards arrive with state-of-the-art preparation nowadays.

Looks like he wants to grab even more

You will need to remove the wax from used boards to make repairs or to structure the base. Structuring or texturing the base is unnecessary for recreational and freestyle snowboarders. A competition racer may want to take the board to a pro shop to have it machine ground or sanded and perhaps "rilled." Rilling involves putting very small furrows the length of the board. For top-level racing such esoteric efforts have been shown to slightly reduce surface friction in some, especially wet, snow conditions.

Back to reality. Your first goal is simply to make sure that the base is flat. A few early models had convex or concave bases, and these should be preserved as the manufacturer intended. For modern snowboards, use a large straightedge that overlaps the sides of the board. Pull it along from tip to tail. If you detect any scuffs, bumps, or high points, even them out with a flat file. If you find any gouges, fill them in and scrape and file them down until the base is again flat and smooth. If your bases are made of regular P-tex, gouges can be filled with a P-tex candle available from any ski shop. To do this, you light the end of the stick with a match, rotate it against a metal scraper to eliminate as much burning carbon as possible, and—keeping it hot—run the molten P-tex into the gouge.

If your board has the UHMW sintered P-tex, drip candle repairs will not work as well without practice. Serious gouges in these bases can be repaired using polyethylene base irons, welders, or repair guns/extruders. The safest way to repair these is to take your board to an experienced shop where they can fix it easily and quickly.

A temporary quick fix for small gouges is to fill them with wax. However, this is only worthwhile psychologically, or if you are trying to sell a used board. Small gouges are imperceptible when riding your board. Another small tip is that prolonged sunshine (UV light) degrades P-tex.

De-Tuning the Edges

The edges on a new board actually have to be de-tuned a little bit. This amounts to slightly dulling or rounding the edges along the nose and tail sections, not along the main running sides. Since a board only has about 40 percent as much edge as a pair of skis, you need all the edge you can get. However, a sharp edge on the shovel (tip) increases the likelihood of catching an edge and "railing out" (getting thrown sideways). Racers may want to de-tune only the most forward nose section, while strict freestylers may want to go back slightly farther than all-around snowboarders would. De-tuning is simple to do, so don't get carried away. Just run a file or whetstone the required length while holding it at a 45-degree angle to the base. Use a finishing stone to remove any burrs. Hold the finishing stone fairly flat instead of tilted. It is all right to have an abrupt change between the slightly dulled section and the sharp section. De-tuning the edges is a one-time operation. Sharpening the working section of the board is what counts.

Beveling the Edges

Another way edges can be prepared for freestyle is to bevel them. A number of manufacturers do this at the factory for their

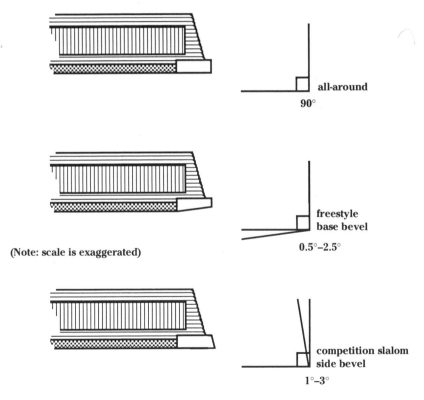

all-around
90°

(Note: scale is exaggerated)

freestyle
base bevel
0.5°–2.5°

competition slalom
side bevel
1°–3°

Figure 10. Edge bevels

freestyle models. Beveling typically only amounts to a microscopic one or two degrees. Think twice about customizing your edges in such a fashion if factory specifications for your board are for flat base edges. True, you can initiate turns more easily with beveled edges, but they will not hold a carve as well. It is impossible to replace steel once you have removed it.

You can also customize edges with a side bevel to increase their holding power. Most boards come with a 90-degree side edge, which is fine for recreational, downhill, and freestyle riding. But for competition slalom you may (or may not) want to subtract two or three degrees (one or two degrees for GS) from the side edge.

Special equipment is required to bevel edges correctly. Larger ski shops can do it, and they may also sell special file holders for hand use that can be precisely adjusted for the exact angle. Such holders are handy even if you want the standard 90 degrees.

If you do not have a ski-type file holder, fix your vice, clamps, and jigs so that you can run a truly square sharp edge perpendicular to the base. And don't forget to de-burr the edge lightly with a stone as the final step. When both edges will shave a thumbnail, it is time to wax.

Waxing

In the fourth dimension, time, snow is not frozen. It is alive. Even a single flake is constantly changing. It is changing even before it falls. It begins as an embryonic crystal, grows, falls, melts, collides, breaks up, and joins together before ever hitting the ground. On the ground, it does not just lie there. It breathes, condenses, evaporates, melts, solidifies, sublimates, and links. It does this nonstop. Like the pseudopods of an amoeba, the tips of the snow crystal are the most active.

The structure of snow varies with its age. New, sharply crystalline snow or snow that is very cold needs a harder wax to prevent the snow from physically gouging the wax, on a micro-

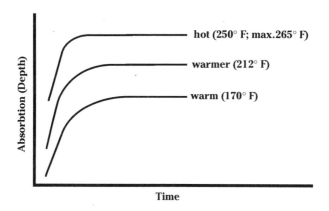

Figure 11. Waxing

scopic scale, which reduces the glide. Older snow has rounded edges, and warmed or sun-exposed snow requires a softer wax. Softer waxes lose less energy to friction. For speeds below 50 mph (that is, anything but downhill racing), optimize your glide by following the charts specifically created for the brand of wax you are using. If you hit speeds of over 50 mph, use a softer wax than the charts suggest. If the snow contains free water or slush, as from rain, mix a silicon additive wax in with your regular wax.

You can apply wax by spraying, rubbing, rolling, painting, or smearing. But for the best results, iron it in hot. Liquid wax can penetrate invisible pore spaces in the polyethylene base structure. The base structure will actually swell like a sponge, although you cannot see this swelling. Later, this wax will slowly work its way to the surface as the outermost wax is worn away on the slopes.

You want your board to soak in as much wax as possible so that you do not have to go through all the trouble of waxing it again soon. The wax must be as warm as possible for as long as it takes to apply it. The warmer the wax is, the "runnier" it will be, and the greater the absorption. You must continue ironing for at least a few minutes to achieve maximum saturation. With these principles in mind, note that the upper limit on wax temperature is about 265° F (130° C). Above that you start to ruin the wax. If the wax starts to "smoke," you are breaking it down with excessive heat. Likewise if the base gets too hot, you may melt the polyethylene and ruin your expensive board. Excessive heat can also harm thermoresins used in laminating the board. Polyethylene melts at about 300° F (150° C).

The two rules to follow are:

✦ Never place an iron on the base of a snowboard without a layer of wax between them.
✦ Never let the wax smoke.

The convenient way to wax a board is to take it to a ski or snowboard shop and have someone else do it. To do it yourself, you need the following equipment: an iron (household variety or an official "waxing iron"), a scraper, and a Scotchbrite® or Fibertex® pad. An indestructible work area is desirable too, since melted wax and wax shavings will end up everywhere, including in carpets.

Most professionals prefer melting the wax on with a special electric wax heater or applying it molten from a pot with a brush. While this latter method works fine, you will never be able to use the brush for any other task again, and it wastes some wax. Another possibility is to melt the wax all over the iron's surface and then generously drip it over the base area. Whatever method you use to get the wax on, do not let the hot iron touch the dry base.

Melt the wax into one sector of your board at a time. Keep the iron moving, however slowly, and watch to see that the base and wax are warm enough to allow good penetration. Ease off or adjust the iron if any smoking occurs. Since the areas near the edges receive the most abuse, they need waxing the most.

After thoroughly treating all areas, let the board cool for twenty to thirty minutes before scraping. This is important.

Scraping merely involves pulling a straightedge along the length of the board, using overlapping strokes until all the visible wax is removed. The direction you pull the edge does not matter. You may feel like you are defeating all of your previous work, but it is important to be thorough. Save the scrapings in a pot or in a ball for the next time. Never polish or buff the waxy surface.

Texture the immeasurably thin layer of wax remaining with a Scotchbrite® or Fibertex® pad or a stiff nylon brush. With this

Snowboard
Maintenance Checklist

✦ To test whether a snowboard needs waxing, run a finger-nail along the base. If there is no residue, it is time for more wax. The base should feel "soapy." The sides may dry up sooner than the center section.

✦ Periodically check the bindings for loose nuts, bolts, and screws, but do not overtighten them. Use Locktite® or a similar product on the threads, but be careful. Such products may destroy plastics.

✦ When storing the board for the summer, apply wax generously, but do not scrape it off as usual. Permit the wax to cover the steel edges. Store the board vertically, heel down, or in a position that will not affect the camber or permit twisting or warping. Avoid strong temperature fluctuations and sunlight.

✦ Check the camber to see if a board has become "fa-tigued" (that is, less responsive). Camber is very slight in snowboards, though, so it may be difficult to tell visually. Foam-core (polyurethane) snowboards are the most susceptible to fatigue, even though they are very tough.

✦ At the first sign of delamination, take a snowboard to a pro shop. There are "miracle" glues available.

finishing touch, your board is truly primed and ready to make fat tracks on the slopes.

Boots

Styles of Snowboarding Boots

Before choosing a pair of boots, you must answer some basic questions about the style of riding you intend to do. There are two kinds of boots to choose from—the style you buy depends on your riding style on the slopes. Soft boots are well suited for soft snow and for maximum flexibility in freestyle maneuvers. Hard boots are better suited for hard snow and for responsive edge control at higher speeds. To be sure, you can "rip" in soft boots and contort in hard-shelled boots, but this is not the optimal way to go. Also, your boot style will determine the type of binding you will use.

The reasons for two boot styles are both historical and geographical. In the United States, skateboarding is a common link among younger snowboarders, so freestyle maneuvers hold priority status. The tweaks, bones, and contorted extensions of freestyle demand severe ankle flexions. For these tricks a soft boot is a natural choice. Also, the original "low-tech" snowboarders in the United States used what was most available, namely, plain winter boots. Any other type of boot in the primitive rubber bindings was pointless anyway, since the original board designs were not designed for packed snow.

As the sport has evolved, a downhiller today blazing through an icy course demands something tougher. European riders, who come from a stronger skiing tradition, have always preferred hard, ski-style boots. In the past, 95 percent of American riders have opted for the soft boots. Now the trend is for more hard-shelled boots. This trend will persist, as innovations for side-to-side flex, adjustable forward tilt, tongue stiffness, and other customizing options continue to become available. No other area of snowboarding is undergoing such intense development, and there are many opportunities for innovation.

So what to do? The fundamental problem is that free-spirited recreationalists like snowboarders want to do it all or, at least, to be able to try. One solution is to have a garage full of boards and boots—like a pro. But all that equipment is expensive and inconvenient. The solution that has evolved is to provide some stiffening reinforcement for the soft boots and to increase the flexibility of the hard-shelled boots.

Soft Boots

One attraction that has pulled long-suffering alpine skiers over to snowboarding is the prospect of spacious, warm, soft boots. Unfortunately, this dream remains unrealized. Unmodified soft boots are more comfortable for walking than ski boots, but they are unsuitable for mean, rigorous snowboarding. The modern pac-boot or "Sorel™" consists of a rubber shoe to which is sewn a water-repellant, high-top leather or nylon canvas upper boot. They are big enough to accommodate removable felt liners, which provide the main insulation.

If you have the money, you can buy true snowboarding boots. These are pac-boots in which the felt inner liners have been replaced by a reinforcing inner boot. This inner boot laces, velcros, or fits snugly enough that your heel will not lift. A nonlifting heel is a basic requirement for fitting all types of ski boots.

If you do not have the money, or if you are simply unwilling to invest much in the early stages, you can fake it. Many have. Cheaper pac-boots are available at discount and Army-Navy type stores. Even cheaper ski boots are available at secondhand stores. There is a glut of old ski boots nowadays because recent binding requirements have made many older boots obsolete. So take out the bladder (inner boot) and possibly the tongue from the ski boot and pitch the shell. Remove the felt liner from the

Snowboarding boot with reinforced liner

Sorel™, slit the tongue if necessary, and insert the ski boot bladder. Voilà! You have a homemade snowboarding boot. A little more padding, trimming, stiffening, and duct taping, and you will have either a mess or a masterpiece.

Do not unnecessarily expose these boots to direct heat or to prolonged sunlight. The rubber will deteriorate after many years, although preservative sprays will help prolong its life. For the leather to last as long as the rubber, treat it periodically with a waterproofing compound. Remember to remove the bladders from the boots after using them, just as you would the felt liners, to let them dry overnight.

Avoid using conventional hiking boots because snowboard bindings are not designed for them; the boot tops are not high enough or strong enough for safe ankle support. They are usually not warm enough, either. Also avoid "moon" boots. They are totally mushy and the bindings will chew up your ankles.

Finally, because of the binding configuration, large, soft boots can sometimes overhang the sides of your board. If they do—

Features of Soft Boots

+ comply with the most common bindings
+ have a comfortable fit that is easily obtained
+ are less expensive than hard boots (especially with ingenuity)
+ permit a "surfer" feel of the board for freestyle maneuvers
+ can be used for other outdoor activities
+ are easy to customize and repair
+ identify you as a snowboarder

and you do not want to change the angle of the bindings—carefully shave and bevel the heels of the boots and position the bindings so that the toes overhang slightly more than the heels. Toes are bendable, but heels are rigid and if these dig in they can lever the board up and off its edge during severe angulation on icy, boilerplate conditions.

Hard-Shelled Boots

As soft boots are becoming stiffer, hard-shelled boots are becoming softer. Originally snowboarders used regular alpine ski boots or hard plastic mountaineering boots. Now ski boot manufacturers (primarily European firms with long experience) are modifying the same basic designs and adding adjustable flex systems. The front boot can even be higher or stiffer than the rear one. It is primarily the front foot that requires the strength, while the rear one needs the greater range of motion. Modern hard boots have an abundance of adjustment options. The fancy hard-shelled boots cost about the same as better ski boots. Try

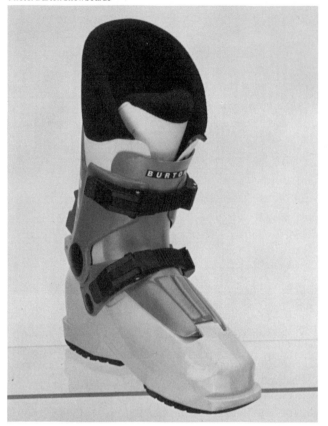

Hard boot

out some hard-shelled boots if you can before deciding on your boot/binding system. It is possible to successfully use some regular ski boots in some high-back bindings. You might be able to try this for insights into the pros and cons of hard-shelled boots.

Both types of boots have proven themselves workable. If your boots are warm and comfortable and do what you want them to do, that is as good as it gets. Rent or borrow and experiment for yourself.

Features of Hard Boots

✦ give superior control for speed
✦ give greater ankle support
✦ are extremely durable
✦ are easier to get in and out of bindings
✦ eliminate binding pressure points
✦ come in flashy colors
✦ do not obviously identify you as a snowboarder

Bindings

Your choice of bindings depends on your choice of boots. Just as selecting a boot style defines the binding style, selecting a binding style can also define the boot style. Manufacturers are working with the American Society for Testing and Materials (ASTM) to standardize bindings. As this process is incomplete, selecting a board may also define the bindings—not necessarily the style of binding but maybe the specific brand.

In the past, manufacturers typically offered only one plate binding and one buckle (high-back) binding. Bindings were not universally interchangeable between different boards because of non-standard hole patterns. For some brands of snowboards or for older used equipment, it was strictly a package deal.

Since bindings (and boots) are so important to your safety and enjoyment, evaluate and compare the bindings when choosing your equipment. A vastly superior binding on a slightly inferior board may be a better deal than the reverse. Test them out and prove or disprove it for yourself. It is not unusual to improve bindings with personalized customizing.

High-back binding

High-Back Bindings

Originally high-back or buckle bindings evolved from designs similar to water-ski bindings. Part of their continuing appeal may subconsciously be that they are different from regular ski bindings.

High-back bindings are constructed of plastic. Some have base plates of nylon, polyamide, aluminum, or polyethylene; some have backs that fold down for transport and storage. The most important differences among models, though, are the number of straps and the way they fasten.

High-back bindings come in two specialized forms. The heavy-duty version is for alpine snowboard skiing and is characterized by a deeply curved back with a shin strap for extra support and strength. Similar but lighter versions for freestyle riding lack a shin strap, and the back is shallow so that lateral motion is not restricted. Some models can be configured either way. Opinions on the virtues of shin straps vary, but you will appreciate shin straps for high-speed carving or when trying to hold a long toe-side traverse at the end of the day. Some two-strap versions include a "tongue" plate to add support and help relieve pressure points. The best solution for pressure points, however, is to have stiff inner bladders in your boots as described in the section on boots (page 118).

The fasteners on the straps are of two types. One type feeds a serrated strap into a spring-loaded ratchet. These are the most secure and reliable, and they permit slightly finer adjustments. Their disadvantage is that they are less convenient, slower to get out of, and cumbersome for hands enclosed in fat gloves or mittens.

The second type of fastener consists of steel bails that engage open, hooked slots. These are very elementary and easy to use. Their disadvantage is that the bails can unexpectedly pop out. If you are skating along with only one foot lightly buckled, and if you stomp the board, your foot may pop out of the binding. Jumps can also pop bails that do not have a stranglehold. Some bindings compromise and use the ratchet style for the crucial ankle straps and bails for the other straps.

Plate Bindings

As with hard boots, Europe has been the domain for plate bindings. There are many brands, but the basic design consists of a rigid plate with large steel bails on each end that clamp onto the toe and heel extensions of the hard-shelled boot. Either the toe or the heel bail may hold the locking lever. With a single flip up or down, you are instantly in or out of the binding. Convenient. Automatic step-in versions are also available.

Plate bindings are constructed of stainless steel, plastic, and sometimes aluminum components. They are relatively lightweight. As mentioned above, plate bindings are becoming

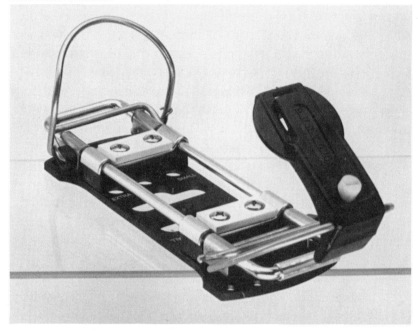

Plate binding

more popular. Rental shops prefer them because they are much easier to adjust.

Plate binding manufacturers have had mixed success in incorporating flexibility mechanisms into the binding. These side-to-side rocking mechanisms may be rigid or consist of rubber pads under the bases.

Mounting Bindings

Three separate geometries affect the position of your bindings: centering them across the board; the angles; and the stance separation distance.

Features of Snowboard Bindings

✦ Both types of snowboard bindings are non-releasable. If only one binding should release, the retained leg could be badly injured. As the statistics show (see section on safety, page 141), keeping both knees aligned and mutually supportive is a relatively safe configuration. Releasable bindings are being developed and tested.

✦ Both types of bindings can sometimes be improved by adding a small canting (tilting) wedge on the rear binding to tip the foot and leg into a slight, forward position towards the front of the board. Such canting improves carving stance and boning.

✦ Wedges for beveling, tilting the heel up towards the toe, are also available. They improve heel-side edging.

✦ Both types adjust to fit a wide range of boot sizes.

✦ Both types cost about the same. Plate bindings might be a little more expensive, especially if you consider them in combination with the hard-shell boots.

✦ Both types are durable and will last indefinitely.

✦ All bindings have safety straps for use at ski resorts.

Centering

Centering the bindings from side-to-side is easy. The only special consideration is that some people prefer their weight very slightly biased towards the toe side. This is solely personal preference. If your boots are so large that they hang over the edges, have them slightly overhang the toe edge, not the heel edge. This is less likely to lever the board up and off its edge in a steep bank. Also, to minimize overhang, the heels can be carefully trimmed or the mounting angles turned more forward.

Centering the bindings fore and aft (on the long axis) is strictly a function of the board's design, and you should follow the manufacturer's recommendations. There is a little latitude in the positioning of the bindings, especially the rear one. Your weight should be centered quite close to the middle of the running surface on modern boards.

Angling

The average angles of 40 to 45 degrees for the front binding and 20 to 25 degrees for the rear binding are good for all-around snowboarding. Freestylers are likely to select smaller angles that are more perpendicular to the sides of the board, especially for the rear foot. Besides making it easier to do Fakies, a more perpendicular stance improves balance and side-to-side strength. For others, the trend is to face forwards, following the lead of Europeans and racers. This position allows the use of narrower boards which are more responsive to edge-to-edge changes. Forward angling improves forward visibility and helps you streamline your profile. It also exaggerates the difference in the toe-to-heel weight shift position. This, in turn, has inspired the design of asymmetrical boards. Forward angling also discourages the swiveling action of the hips and rear leg as seen in skidded turns. Instead it encourages carved turns.

Stance Separation

Your stance separation distance depends on your leg length and personal preference. Advanced and hard-boot riders often use narrower stances that are more compatible with the more-forward mounting angles. A narrower stance centers your weight better for carving turns and achieving faster speeds. A wider stance gives you more stable balance and reduces the apparent swing weight of the board—both of which are important for freestylers.

Attaching

Two methods are used for attaching bindings. One method uses pre-drilled holes with steel inserts. Screw-headed bolts then precisely align the bindings at fixed angles. A wide range of adjustment is possible. Besides being simple, this method has the advantage of easily allowing you to change stance angles or to change from a goofy to a regular stance (and vice versa).

A second method follows the ski-industry standard of having the purchaser drill holes for sheet-metal screws. An aluminum plate under the top layer of the board provides the holding strength. Manufacturers supply directions, but if you have any concerns about over-drilling or misalignment, have it done professionally. If you purchase your new board from a snowboarding shop, they will normally do it for you without charge. This method is less expensive to manufacture and allows you to place the bindings exactly where you want them.

Accessories

Apparel

Snowboarders and alpine skiers face a difficult problem. Bursts of demanding activity are followed by periods of inactivity when one is exposed to cold, snow, and especially wind. To fight these conditions a clothing scheme that includes a moisture-wicking underlayer, a midlayer of insulation, and an outer layer of wind/waterproofing has become standard.

The best undergarments are made with synthetics. Polypropylene is very good, though it can shrink. Newer fibers produced under trade names such as *Thermax, Terylene,* and *Caprilene* have received excellent reviews. New names appear each season. Silk is not warm and can stretch. Wool is itchy. Cotton is the worst by far, since it holds all moisture. It should be banished except for summertime wear. Blue jeans restrict leg motion in the extreme, especially when they're wet—and they always get cold and wet.

Midlayer fabrics can be of various materials and thicknesses depending upon conditions. Wool is a standard. Synthetics are the choice among many skiwear manufacturers. Goose-down vests and parkas are wonderfully light and warm *if* they stay dry. But for snowboarders that is a nearly impossible *if*. Bulk is directly associated with insulative value. However the newer breathable outer fabrics have changed the rules. To expel the moisture wicked from the skin, the water must be evaporated by body heat and then diffused through the outer shell. The thinner the garments are, the easier and faster this process can take place. So look for well-designed winter garments that have thick insulation where it is needed and thin insulation where it is not needed, like under the arms. Look for vents and mesh. Also look for lots of big, easy-working zippers.

The standard nylon shells have been replaced with "waterproof/breathables." These are great if you do not expect as much from them as the price tag may suggest. During hard work, expect no more than 50 percent of the moisture at most to transpire through the fabric.

The water-repellant layer of waterproof/breathables does deteriorate, so periodically treat it with a silicon spray. Several layers sprayed on over several days are preferable to one big soak. In fact, do *not* literally soak the material by using the laundry-type refurbishers or the inner lining will then be treated, and it will fight moisture exchange from the inside. Scotchgard® and Zepel® are recognized brands of silicon sprays. For a simple test, water will bead up on new or properly conditioned material.

Rider: Zach Bingham Photo: Mike Hatchett

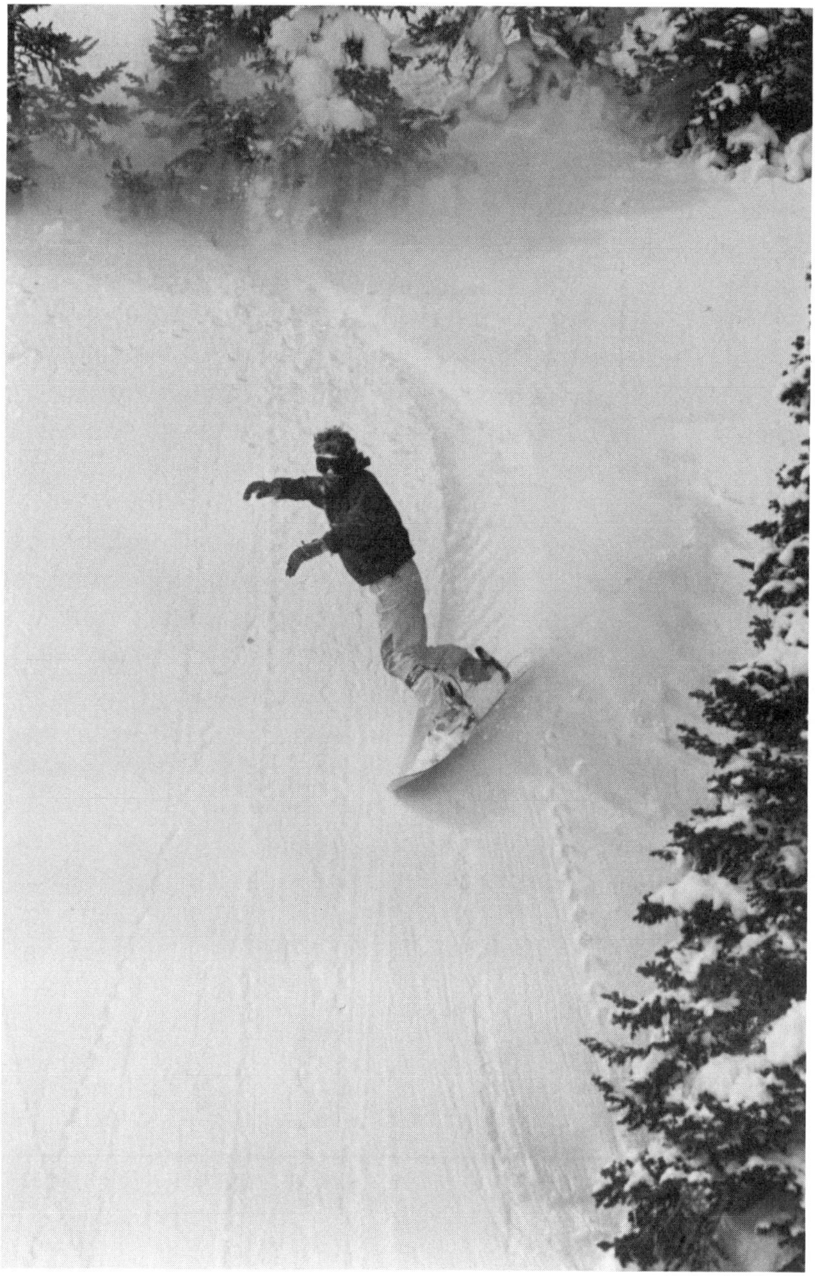

Eyewear

You may think eyewear a trivial subject. However, one university study reported that athletes who wore special PX-2000 lenses increased their learning and performance of gross motor skills by 33 percent over six weeks compared to the control group. This study was for tennis players, but snowboarders are exposed to far more rigorous conditions. Compared to the control group, the study found that those using the special lenses experienced less glare, less hazardous UV light, less eye fatigue, and enhanced contrast and depth perception.

In order of increasing protection, your choices include: sport glasses (sunglasses), sport shields, and goggles. Glasses, of course, have the monopoly on correcting vision. Use retainers on sunglasses. Tight retainers are more secure than the "hang loose" style. Shields combine style, convenience, and function, and will no doubt remain popular among snowboarders. Goggles give you maximum protection, not just for wind and snow but also for cold. When conditions are really miserable, they are the best choice. Some models are designed to fit over glasses.

Don't think the book ends here even though the next section is labeled an "Appendix." There is a wealth of information "in them thar pages"—maybe some of the most valuable information of all!

· Back Country Considerations

Cold

In nature, what is the number-one killer of people outdoors? Lightning. What is the number-one killer of outdoors people? Hypothermia. Lowered body temperatures caused by cold—and usually by wetness, too—result in loss of energy, loss of coordination, and loss of mental acuteness. This process feeds back on itself with more poor thinking and decision making, inability to work zippers and small matches, and fatigue. This results in more chilling. In the end, the heart stops, but the process generally becomes irreversible long before then. Frostbite is nothing compared to hypothermia. Your toes may slowly decay into blackened stubs, but you live. Hypothermia kills. If you start to shiver, consider it an emergency and act accordingly while you still have the sense and ability to do so. The key to both maladies is prevention.

Thirst is not always recognizable under cold conditions, but dehydration can be a hidden source of fatigue, and performance can drop. Remember that alcohol will increase both fluid loss and heat loss. A little fresh snow is OK, if you have the body heat to spare.

Snowboarding Out of Bounds

Unquestionably, wonderful runs exist far from the beaten slopes. But the price you have to pay for taking them is exposure to two life-threatening dangers—getting lost and avalanches. If you have hiked in, in the true mountaineer's style, you are unlikely to get lost. But if you venture illegally out of a ski area's boundary, your chances of getting lost are high. If the drainages ran back to civilization at the bottom, they would not have been placed out of bounds to begin with—unless there are cliffs, dead ends, or avalanche problems. Something is wrong. So pick your own mountain for back-country riding and not the ski area's.

Avalanches are everyone's nightmare, but skiers and snowboarders really ask for it. The problem is that the most attractive places to rip are fairly steep, open slopes, possibly with natural half-pipes. And the most attractive times are just after storms while the snow is still untouched. These are avalanche conditions. Shallow slopes and steep cliffs are actually safer than are the moderately steep slopes. Also safer are slopes with dense stands of trees. A beautiful half-pipe gully may be nothing more than an avalanche chute in disguise. Most avalanches, if they did not release during the storm, cut loose shortly afterwards. Leeward slopes are generally more dangerous than windward slopes. In midwinter, north-facing slopes are the most likely to slide. On sunny spring days, south-facing slopes are the more dangerous. Snow crystal types and previous temperature patterns are also important. There are so many aspects to understanding avalanches that the prospective back country snowboarder should read Tony Daffern's classic *Avalanche Safety for Skiers and Climbers* (Calgary, Alberta: Rocky Mountain Books, 1986) or other similar books.

APPENDIX B

Snowboarding History

People have been trying to stand up and go down snowy hills on everything from planks to linoleum sheets to "official" toboggans for longer than anyone knows.

The Scandinavians are credited with developing a method for traveling on snow. They invented skis as a means for "walking" over flat, snow-covered ground. Naturally, downhill skiers inherited the tradition: one board for each foot. The first downhill skiers compensated for the awkwardness of this method by using a single balancing pole carried in the fashion of a circus performer. A rock pictograph in Norway painted around 2000 B.C. shows the technique used in primitive skiing. Skis preserved in the flat peat bogs of Sweden and Finland are 500 years older than that.

Technologically, snowboarding is most closely allied with skiing, though it is not from skiing that most snowboard riders have come to the sport. Some come from surfing, which can trace its technological lineage back to the ancient Polynesians of Hawaii, and others from skateboarding, which can trace its technological origins to the nineteenth century at best. Both sports have aided in snowboarding's conceptual evolution though.

Snowboarding had its official birth in the mid-1960s when Sherman Poppen shaped a plywood board with an upturned nose for sledding on snow. (His very first model was made from two short skis.) A noteworthy feature of his "Snurfer," as it came to be called, was a hand-held rope leading to the nose of the board.

From 1966 to 1981 progress was irregular and definitely "low-tech," but improvements in board materials, design, and construction went steadily forward. In the early 1980s, manufacturers added metal edges and adopted the relatively "high-tech" ideas of the ski industry. Snowboard design and construction quickly improved and have now reached a high and comparatively stable standard. Though the growth of snowboard technology is leveling off, it will never stop.

The achievements of snowboarders continue to grow, too. Snowboarders have assailed peaks such as Kilimanjaro, Aconcagua, the Matterhorn, the Eiger, and those in the Himalayas. Speed records are constantly being nudged forward. With the new aerospace materials constantly becoming available and with the assistance of computer-aided design and manufacturing, who knows what the future will hold?

APPENDIX C

Who Snowboards

Here are some statistics from readership surveys made by the *TransWorld SNOWboarding, International Snowboard,* and *Snowboarder* magazines and by the North American Snowboard Association (NASBA). Their numbers are inconsistent, so the information is given as ranges.

Regional Activity
(Percentage of Magazine Subscriptions)

East	25 to 34%
Midwest	11 to 18%
West	24 to 51%
Canada	11 to 16%

The average age of survey respondents is between 18 and 19 with 20 percent to 24 percent of the riders adults (21 years old and over). The average age and the percentage of adult participants are both increasing as more parents and older skiers are learning how simple and exciting snowboarding can be.

The percentage of female participants may be 2 percent, 8 percent, or 25 percent. Take your pick. The only certainty is that the number of female snowboarders is increasing.

Snowboarders' Involvement in Other Sports
(Percentage of Survey Respondents)

Skateboarding	46 to 77%
Skiing (alpine)	40 to 60%
Surfing	17 to 31%
Sailboarding	4 to 25%

Rider: Jeff Van Kleeck   Photo: Joe Dockery

Midway through a BFM

Other popular interests of the survey respondents include biking (mountain and BMX), waterskiing, and aquatic sports. The feelings in the industry are that skateboarders will continue to be a core group, that there will be increased crossover from downhill skiing, and that surfers are a fairly isolated group.

Ability or Experience Profile
(Percentage of Survey Respondents)

Beginner (1 year or less)	36 to 55%
Intermediate (2 years)	20 to 44%
Expert (3 or more years)	17 to 24%

Preferred Conditions
(Percentage of Survey Respondents)

Powder	40%
Half-pipe	26%
Groomed	11%
All	8%
Moguls	6%
Other	9%

APPENDIX D

Safety

Injury Statistics

For snowboarding to be allowed at ski resorts, decision makers needed to know the relative dangers of snowboarding compared to downhill skiing. The two best-known studies are "Snowboarding Injuries on Alpine Slopes" by Jasper E. Shealy and Paul D. Sundman (*Skiing Trauma and Safety,* American Society for Testing and Materials [ASTM] Special Technical Publication 1022, pages 75–81) and "Snowboard Injuries" by Dr. Edward C. Pino and Dr. Mark R. Colville (*The American Journal of Sports Medicine,* Volume 17, No. 6, November-December 1989, pages 778–81). The main results of these research efforts are shown in the following tables and graphs. All of the snowboarding data are preliminary and based on smaller samples and collected over a shorter period than the data for alpine skiing.

Table 1. Characteristics of Injured Skiers
(Percentage of Survey Respondents)

	Snowboard Skiing	*Alpine Skiing*
Median age	19 years	19 years
Percentage male	90.7	60.0
Weight	135 pounds	128 pounds

Source: Shealy and Sundman, "Snowboarding Injuries on Alpine Slopes"

The impression from Table 1 that snowboarders are heavier than skiers is quite possibly backwards. More likely, the average weights reflect the different male/female ratios.

Table 2. Injuries by Skill Level
(Percentage of Survey Respondents)

Skill Level	Snowboard Skiing	Alpine Skiing
Beginner	55.3%	33.9%
Low Intermediate		15.3%
Intermediate	29.8%	33.1%
Advanced	10.6%	11.6%
Expert		6.2%
Unclassified	4.3%	
Number of injuries per 1000 days	4.2	3.2

Source: Shealy and Sundman, "Snowboarding Injuries on Alpine Slopes"

Table 2 suggests that the injury rate declines faster with experience for snowboarders than for skiers. Many skiers have years of experience compared to most snowboarders and so have outgrown the high-injury-rate brackets (beginner and low intermediate). Most snowboarders, in contrast, have only a few years of experience. This may explain the implication that snowboarders can expect about one more injury in a thousand days of activity (about two injuries per lifetime).

The insurance companies for the ski resorts concluded that there was no significant difference in the danger of injuries to downhill skiers and to snowboard skiers. In fact, the studies suggest that snowboarding injuries tend to be less serious than those from skiing.

Table 3. Types of Injuries
(Percentage of Survey Respondents)

Injury	Snowboard Skiing	Alpine Skiing
Fracture	13.6%	19.1%
Dislocation	5.1%	5.5%
Strain/Sprain	64.4%	48.4%
Laceration	1.1%	14.6%
Contusion (Bruising)	11.9%	11.9%
Other	3.6%	0.5%

Source: Shealy and Sundman, "Snowboarding Injuries on Alpine Slopes"

This information should be compared with that of Pino and Colville. The Pino and Colville study used a larger sample size (267 vs. 59) and was more recent (1986–87 vs. 1985–86). The Pino and Colville sample also included more advanced snowboarders (49 percent intermediate and 36 percent expert with only 15 percent beginners). Table 4 is a corresponding table based on their data.

Table 4. Types of Injuries
(Percentage of Survey Respondents)

Fracture	24.6%
Ligament sprain	26.4%
Muscle strain	4.5%
Laceration	3.6%
Contusion	11.8%
Other	29.1%

Source: Pino and Colville, "Snowboard Injuries"

The "other" category in the Pino and Colville study is disconcertingly large and suspicious. Snowboarding has a deserved reputation for falls in which one's head or face hits the snow. It is unclear if these injuries are included in the "other" category. It is no surprise that the probability of laceration is lower, since a snowboard is never free to "windmill" like a released ski.

The constraints of the study prevented Pino and Colville from calculating a true injury rate per rider per day, but their overall estimate was 41 injuries per 100 snowboarders during their careers. This means that the average rider would have had to have been out snowboarding 103 days in order to show the same values as Shealy and Sundman. This is a very doubtful average, since almost 30 percent of the riders had fewer than 20 days' experience. If the average were a more realistic 50 days, the injury rate would be twice that given by Shealy and Sundman. All in all, it appears that snowboarding for experienced riders is similar to skiing in terms of safety, but that there

Table 5. Snowboarding vs. Alpine Skiing Injuries
(Percentage of Survey Respondents)

Part of Body Injured	Snowboard* Skiing	Snowboard** Skiing	Alpine* Skiing
Hand, face & trunk	12.3%	18.2%	15%
Shoulders	8.8%	11.8%	7%
Arm and elbow	3.6%	4.5%	9%
Wrist, hand & fingers	16.9%	12.7%	11%
Lower trunk & legs	8.8%	11.8%	16%
Knees	15.8%	11.8%	27%
Ankle & foot	36.7%	29.1%	18%
Upper body	35.6%	47.3%	41%
Lower body	59.3%	52.7%	59%
Other	5.1%		

Sources: *Shealy and Sundman, "Snowboarding Injuries on Alpine Slopes"
**Pino and Colville, "Snowboard Injuries"

are distinct differences in the patterns of injury. Snowboarding per-haps has relatively fewer major injuries reported. Specifically, knee injuries seem proportionately less likely.

The evidence is clear: you must be prudent and lucky in order to escape injury, especially in the early learning stages.

What are common injuries to snowboarders and how can you prevent them?

Given the uncertainty of the statistics in Table 5, only a few con-clusions are safe. The skiing data are the most reliable. From them, one can claim that for skiing the lower body takes the most abuse and much of this is focused on the knees. For snowboarding, knee injuries appear to be about half as likely as for skiing, while ankle injuries are about twice as likely. Foot injuries make up only 10 to 15 percent of the cases in the ankle and foot category. Evidence suggests that you can reduce your chances of injury to your legs, especially your ankles, by wearing hard-shelled boots or strongly reinforced soft boots. Although this seems to make sense, the data are biased by the fact that more experienced boarders are more likely to use stiffer boots. Experience alone may effect reduction in the injury rate.

Not having poles, snowboarders have fewer thumb injuries, but more wrist injuries.

Because of snowboarding's unique stance, it is also instructive to compare injuries to snowboarders' left sides vs. their right sides (Table 6).

Table 6. Injuries by Side of Body
(Percentage of Survey Respondents)

	Left*	Right*	Front**	Back**
Ankle & Foot	62%	38%	80%	20%
Knee	67%	33%	67%	33%
Leg			75%	25%
Wrist & Hand			73%	28%
Shoulder			55%	45%

Sources: *Shealy and Sundman, "Snowboarding Injuries on Alpine Slopes"
**Pino and Colville, "Snowboard Injuries"

If we assume that 30 percent of riders are goofy-footed, the left and right "ankle & foot" injuries translate into 79.8 and 20.2 percent for front and back "ankle & foot" injuries—which is the same as Pino and Colville discovered. The same pattern holds for the knees. The implication is clear. The front side of your body relative to the board needs all the protection it can get.

To clarify the difficulty, put your foot down and keep it flat. You can tilt to the inside about 45 degrees, but to the outside only about half as far (if you don't cheat). If you conscientiously practice stretching and conditioning, though, you can increase your flexibility and reduce your chances of injury. This can hardly be emphasized enough.

About two-thirds of snowboarding injuries are caused by torsion (twisting). These torsional injuries are the ones showing up under knee and ankle problems. What happens? During a forward fall over the shovel of the board (as distinguished from a toe-side fall over the side of the board), the front ankle is crunched forwards and sideways (hyperdorsiflexion). This causes crushing and pulling injuries to the ankle and sprains of the ligaments and of the Achilles' tendon.

What causes such falls? Common causes of a forward fall are: crashing from a jump (wrong body position, off-balance, or shallow landing zone), suddenly hitting heavy snow or a pit, or losing control in a mogul field. In a sideways fall, impact injuries (for example, bruises and dislocations) are a danger. The ankles are comparatively safe in a sideways fall if the board doesn't twist because there is no long lever to resist their rotation; the board easily tilts with the feet from side to side. The heels or toes normally lift the board up with ease, and so relieve any undue stresses on the ankles. Torsional and bending injuries while having only one foot attached (for example, when getting off a lift) are well known.

How to Prevent Injuries

Forward Falls

What can be done to increase your safety in forward falls? First, remember the potential causes of such falls and always avoid "sucker" jumps (see page 57). If you have a split second when you realize you're going to crash, bend your knees and try to get low (and often forward).

Overbanking over the bank

Your weight (gravity and centrifugal force combined) will automatically be closer to its proper position. You also will not have as far to fall. The forward momentum of your center of gravity will have a shorter lever on which to exert its bending force. You may also inadvertently tip the board so that it spins out and converts a front fall to a side fall. Your knees are less vulnerable bent than they are when straight. However, you do not want your knees fully compressed into a crouch, either. Finally, be sure to reinforce any Sorel™-type boot with a ski boot bladder or wear a strong snowboarding boot. Pino and Colville found for experienced riders that using hard-shell and reinforced boots cut ankle injuries by 50 percent compared to unreinforced soft boots.

Impact Injuries

The analysis behind impact injuries is more obvious. In skateboarding or skiing, there is often the possibility of using one of your legs to partially catch yourself before your upper body hits the ground. With a sideways fall on a snowboard, you can do little to brake your fall. Your arms are simply not designed to catch the full weight and momentum of your body. Half of the fractures reported by Shealy and Sundman were of the wrist, hand, or fingers (others were to the legs; none were to the arms). All of the dislocations were of shoulders.

What causes such falls? Many things, but topping the list is improper edge control. In particular, if you do not hold a dominant edge or if you let the downhill edge catch, you will crash. Catching your heel edge is probably an important cause of concussions. Neither study discusses how many injuries occurred when exiting lifts. But the special danger in this situation is well known; it could contribute to the number of front leg injuries and of fractures without impact.

Sideways Falls

What can be done to increase your safety in sideways falls? Shealy and Sundman advise: "A possible intervention for the hand, wrist, and finger injuries would be to consider the use of poles or to teach riders to not try to catch themselves while falling." Not likely. The instinctive reflex to break a fall can only be overridden easily in powder, but that scarcely counts.

There are other real options. Thanks to hardcore skateboarders, knee pads are acceptable and are well worth using. Your knee-cap is bony; it needs protection. The same can be said for wrist guards. A butt-pad is not as important. Both butt-pads and knee pads have an added virtue, however—they make it more comfortable for resting on the slope while waiting for your buddies to catch up. Some high-class skiwear designed especially for snowboarders has removable elbow, knee, hip, and rear-end pads. Regular knee pads stay in place best if worn underneath pants rather than on the outside.

Getting as low as possible has the same benefits for reducing injuries in sideways falls as in forward falls. Bending the elbow is important. Just as with the knee, bending it will reduce the stress. A locked elbow is guaranteed to create shoulder and wrist trouble.

Your front wrist is in greater danger because it receives the most weight in a fall. In some cases, making a fist will protect your fingers. At the least keep your thumb in. You will feel better about making a fist if you are wearing big, fat, warm mittens or gloves.

This brings up another point. The warmer your muscles, tendons, and ligaments are, the more resistant they will be to injury. For heel-side falls, a judo slap—actively slapping both arms hard into the snow—will reduce the impact on your torso and head.

For toe-side falls, knee-pads will help you to position your fall properly (that is, low). Avoid wearing protective eyewear that might cut or scrape your face.

Backward Falls

The only primary type of fall not yet discussed is a backward fall (as distinguished from a heel-side fall). Although leaning too far back is a major cause of falls, truly backward falls are uncommon. But they can be serious because they involve compression and stretching injuries to the ankles. The crucial point to remember is not to remain upright when falling backwards down the board's long axis. Remaining upright increases the bending forces that can cause injuries. Instead, collapse and convert a potential backwards fall into an uphill side fall, either to the toe side or the heel side.

On steep slopes you will not have as far to fall in the uphill direction. Don't dwell on the other possibility—the extra distance if you were to fall downhill—or you may become timid and keep your weight too far back and so be guaranteed to eat snow. If a panel of judges would rank your fall a "10," your troubles are multiplied. On a steep hill you may start somersaulting. You have to risk opening up immediately before gaining speed and becoming disoriented. Opening up is risky and scary, but the last thing you want to break is your neck. Also if you are speeding along on hardpack, steep or not, and you fall, immediately get the board in the air and off the snow so you slide freely a second rather than catching and being flailed by your board. But then if you do not want to erase yourself over the next 100 yards, you must dig in. You can use your elbows in snow, but your board is the best device for digging in. If you are on boilerplate, you have to dig in with your board. Each situation is unique, but generally burying only one corner of the board is best. This gives you some measure of control. If you put the whole edge down, it is likely to catch, chatter, or oscillate—all of which will do a number on your ankles and the fillings in your teeth. If you are headed for something solid or vertical, get that board planted!

Like everything else in snowboarding, it is possible to become quite skilled, adept, and even clever in learning to crash. Always stay in control. That way you can learn how to fall gradually over a period of time, rather than spectacularly early in your snowboarding career.

Organizations Related to Snowboarding

Associations

AFS   Association Française de Snowboard (Via Masala 16, 37128 Verona, Italy).

ASTM   American Society for Testing and Materials. Helped establish credibility for ski resort acceptance. Now involved in standardization of equipment, such as bindings and mounting.

CSA   Canadian Snowboard Association (609 Denman Street, Vancouver, B.C. V6G-2L3, Canada). Standardization of equipment and certification requirements.

DVDS   Dach Verban der Desterreicheschen Schneesurfer (Kajertanerplatz 4, 5020 Salzburg, Austria).

GSA   German Snowboard Association (Oberer Graben 15, 8900 Augsburg, West Germany).

ISA   International Snowboard Association (P.O. Box 38836, Denver, Colorado).

MWSA   Midwest Snowboard Association (1299 Glover Drive, Xenia, Ohio 45385).

NASBA   North American Snowboard Association (P.O. Box 2522, Durango, Colorado 81302). Sanctioning body for competitions.

NASTAR   National Standard Races (P.O. Box 4580, Aspen, Colorado

81611). Provides "yardstick" races for amateur snowboarders. Awards available.

NSPS   National Ski Patrol System (2901 Sheridan Boulevard, Denver, Colorado 80214). The largest winter rescue organization in the world.

PSIA   Professional Ski Instructors of America (133 South Van Gordon, Suite 240, Lakewood, Colorado 80228). Organization sanctioning teaching and certification programs in skiing and snowboarding.

SSA   Swiss Snowboard Association (Moleson 24, 1630 Bulle, Switzerland).

USASA   United States Amateur Snowboard Association (Box 251, Green Valley Lake, California 92341). Sanctioning body for competitions.

USIA   United Ski Industries Association (P.O. Box 2883, Springfield, Massachusetts 01101). Provides operating protocol for ski areas. Sponsors and promotes the "Skier's Responsibility Code."

English Language Magazines

These are in alphabetic order; all are excellent magazines.

International Snowboard Magazine
Box 170309
San Francisco, California 94117-0309

Snowboarder
Box 1028
Dana Point, California 92629

Snowboarders Edge
P.O. Box 357
Vermont, Victoria 3133
Australia

TransWorld SNOWboarding
Box 3774
Escondido, California 92025

Glossary

ABS	Tough plastic commonly used as the topsheet on snowboards. Acrylonitrite Butadiene Styrene.
Alpine skiing	Downhill skiing at a ski resort. Riding style emphasizing speed.
Backside edge	Heel-side edge.
Bails	Heavy gauge wire loops for fastening bindings.
Base	The P-tex bottom of the board. See diagram, page 108.
Bevel	The angle the edge has relative to the base. Helps to initiate or to hold turns. See diagram, page 113.
Bevel plate/wedge	Shim or wedge to lift the heel of the foot above the toes.
Binding	Device used to fasten feet to snowboard.
Bladder	Inner boot.
Boilerplate	Extremely hardpacked snow or ice.
Bone	Straightening leg to full extension.
Bowl	Concave-shaped slope, usually with few trees.
Bunny slope	Gentle slope for beginning snowboarders.
Camber	Upward bow of the board when viewed from the side. See page 37.
Cant plate/wedge	Shim or wedge to tilt the outside of the foot towards the arch of the foot (and towards the nose of the board when used on the back binding).

Carbon fiber	Graphite fiber. Similar to fiberglass but stronger, a better dampener, and more expensive.
Carving	Turning with weight shift and without skidding.
Chair lift	Ski slope transportation system using chairs suspended from a cable system.
Contact edge	The effective running length of edge on the snow.
Corduroy	Ribbed snow texture as a result of grooming machines.
Cornice	Overhanging mass of snow.
Cracked edges	Segmented edges used in the nose and tail. They help isolate vibration and are not as stiff as continuous edges.
Crud	Snow condition characterized by an irregular surface with large chunks of snow, usually heavy.
Crust	Snow compacted on the surface from sunshine, sleet, or wind.
Electra base	Brand name of low-density P-tex with graphite.
Epoxy	Tough glue used to laminate snowboard layers.
Extruded	Shaped by forcing through a die.
Fall line	Most direct line down a slope. The direction a ball would roll.
Fiberglass	Glass fibers soaked in epoxy or polyester resin. The fundamental strengthening element in most snowboards.
Flex	Bendability or stiffness of snowboard.
Flex pattern	Relative stiffness in front, middle, and rear of board.
Frontside edge	Toe-side edge.
Gondola	Lift using enclosed cabins attached to a cable system.
Goofy-foot	Right-foot-forward stance.
Graphite	Carbon fiber for composite construction.

Groomed	Snow smoothed and compacted to increase its uniformity and persistence.
Halfpipe	Channel between two walls. See diagram, page 64.
Hard-shelled boots	Stiff urethane boots.
Hardpack	Snow compacted by skiers, grooming machines, the weather, and time.
High-back binding	Binding for soft boots. See photograph, page 124.
Horizontal lamination	Construction method of gluing layers like plywood.
Hybrid construction	Built using two or more technologies or materials.
Kevlar	Extremely strong and tough material (Aramid fiber) for reinforcing snowboards. Lighter, harder to work with, and more expensive than graphite.
Kicked tail	Tail with a curve lifting it off the snow.
Mono-ski	Wide ski with both bindings on one ski.
N/cm	Force per length. (Newtons/centimeter.)
P-tex	Brand name of polyethylene used for snowboard base material.
Plate binding	Binding designed for hard-shelled boots. See photograph, page 126.
Platter lift	See Poma lift.
Polyethylene	Versatile, lightweight plastic used for base material on snowboards.
Polypropylene	Versatile, lightweight plastic used in fibrous form for winter garment insulation.
Polyurethane	Versatile, lightweight plastic used in dense form for boot shells and bindings. Used in foam composition for snowboard cores.
Poma lift	Surface tow using a pole with an end disk (platter) attached to a moving cable.
Pony lift	See Poma lift.

Quarterpipe	Halfpipe with only one wall.
Rail	Side edge of snowboard.
Ratchet buckle	Spring-loaded fastener with a sawtooth configuration.
Regular-foot	Left-foot-forward stance.
Responsibility code	Outline of personal responsibilities. The first rule is to ride in control and in such a manner that you can always avoid other people or obstacles.
Reverse camber	Down-bowing of a snowboard from weight.
Rocker	Convex shape to the running surface of a snowboard.
Rope tow	Surface tow using a continuous loop of moving rope.
Safety strap	Required retention strap attaching the board to the rider's leg.
Sailboarding	Windsurfing.
Sandwich	Laminated construction in layers.
Shin-straps	Optional binding straps on some high-backs.
Shovel	Upcurved area at the front of the snowboard. See diagram, page 37.
Shredding	Snowboarding, etc.
Sidecut	Narrowing of the board width in the midsection. Helps to establish turns when carving.
Sideslip	Technique of sliding or skidding down a hill with the board constantly perpendicular to the fall line.
Sidewall	Side of the board.
Sintered	Manufacturing process of forming powdered P-tex mixture into a solid with heat and pressure. Used in making specialized bases.
Skating	Pushing along with the free rear foot.

Ski area boundary	Perimeter of the ski area, beyond which access is not permitted. Out-of-bounds areas are not patrolled or controlled for avalanches.
Skidding	Plowing snow with the board.
Snow	Flaky water. Types of snow include: champagne powder, wind-blown pack, groomed, corn snow, cold smoke, frozen granular, firm, crud, bottomless powder, sugar, machine tilled, crust, hero powder, buffed snow, corduroy, ball bearing, spring snow, ballroom, and virgin powder.
Soft binding	High-back binding. See photograph, page 124.
Surface tow	One of various ski slope transportation systems in which skier is pulled along the surface. Called drag tows in Europe.
Swing weight	The weight and resistance of a board to turning or rotating. Increases with increasing length or thickness.
T-bar	Surface tow consisting of a pole with a crossbar at the end attached to a moving cable.
Tail	Rear or back end of board. See diagram, page 37.
Taper	The narrowing of the tail of a board compared to the nose. Influences turning characteristics.
Titanal	Alloy of titanium and aluminum.
Tongue plate	Protective piece on some high-back bindings between straps and instep of foot.
Torqued	Twisted or levered.
Torsion box	Sophisticated construction method providing a full wrap of reinforcement material around core material.
Torsional rigidity	Resistance to longitudinal twisting.
Transition	Curved section of halfpipe between the flat area and the more vertical wall.

Traverse	Sideways across a slope. Perpendicular to fall line.
Tweak	To push to the limit. To become as distorted as possible.
Urethane	See Polyurethane.
Vertical lamination	Laminating long, narrow strips of wood side by side. Produces a strong, resilient, and durable core.
Wall	The vertical section of a halfpipe.
Waxing	The application of water-repellant materials to the base of the board, which vastly improves speed and turnability.
Wedge	Canting or tilting insert to slant the foot either towards the other foot or forwards towards the toes. See Bevel plate/wedge and Cant plate/wedge.

Index

Numbers in *italics* refer to pages with illustrations.

Bunny slope, 6, 9, 10, 153